On my Knees

Also by Periel Aschenbrand

The Only Bush I Trust Is My Own

On my Knees

A Memoir

PERIEL ASCHENBRAND

HARPER ● PERENNIAL

NEW YORK ● LONDON ● TORONTO ● SYDNEY ● NEW DELHI ● AUCKLAND

HARPER ●PERENNIAL

HarperCollins books may be purchased for educational, business, or sales promotional use. For information please e-mail the Special Markets Department at SPsales@harpercollins.com.

FIRST EDITION

Designed by Michael Correy

Library of Congress Cataloging-in-Publication Data is available upon request.

ISBN 978-0-06-202689-7

13 14 15 16 17   OV/RRD   10 9 8 7 6 5 4 3 2 1

Author's Note

I have changed the names of some individuals, and modified identifying features, including physical descriptions and occupations, of other individuals in order to preserve their anonymity. In some cases, composite characters have been created or timelines have been compressed, in order to further preserve privacy and to maintain narrative flow.

For Guy

Contents

I do not regret the things I have done, but those I did not do.

—MARK TWAIN

SETTING THE STAGE:
THE ANUS IS BACK

Though I grew up in Queens, I try to avoid going back there at all cost. Every time I go I have a totally irrational meltdown that by just going there to *visit*, my worst nightmare will come true and I will somehow get stuck living there for the rest of my life. I haven't lived in Queens since I was seventeen, but it still makes me nervous. If my parents didn't live there, I would have no reason to ever step foot in the largest and most ethnically diverse borough of New York. But alas, my parents do live there and I guess I love my parents more than I hate Queens, so when they call, I come.

I mean, sort of. That's actually kind of a lie. I live in Manhattan and my mother works in Manhattan and though my father is retired, he often drives my mom to work and so we usually meet in Manhattan. But once every four to six months, my mother becomes irate that I never visit them, so I acquiesce. And also, like most things, the anticipation of the thing is worse than the thing itself—which is to say that although Queens is kind of a shithole, it's not that bad once you're there.

Most recently, I was summoned to my parents' house to bathe my parents' pug, Señor. Giving Señor a bath is comprised of putting the dog in the sink, turning on the water, rubbing soap on him, and rinsing him off. For the most part he just stands there, looking at you appreciatively. He's a *pug* not a rottweiler. In other words, a monkey could do this job. But for some reason, my parents think I am the only person who is capable of it, which is typically neurotic of them and totally fucking ridiculous. But my parents are so wonderful and they ask so little of me. So really, what can I do but oblige them?

While washing the dog is easy, the drying part can get tricky. When you try to dry him off, Señor goes totally berserk and tries to steal the towel, and then sometimes he takes off like a bat out of hell and races around the apartment in circles. There is definitely an art to drying him and I'm usually pretty good at it. But this time, he escaped and went completely ballistic. Instead of racing around in circles, he kept making a beeline straight for my behind with such vigor you would have thought he was a bloodhound, hot on the trail of JonBenét Ramsey's remains in my anal cavity. He kept ramming his flat pug face into my ass and every time I turned my body, he raced back right behind me and did it again. I started screaming, "He's trying to give me a rim job!"

My mother: "A *ring job*? What is a ring job?"

Me, continuing to scream: "Not a ring job, Mommy, a *rim* job!"

My mother: "What is a *rim job*?"

Me: "Mommy, how long have you lived in this country? You don't know what a rim job is? How do you not know what a rim job is? A rim job is when you lick someone's anus."

My mother: "Oh my God. I can't believe this. That is *terrible*."

Me: "Terrible? What's terrible about it? There's nothing terrible about a rim job. Don't you know, the anus is back?"

My mother: "The anus is back. *O-kay*. I didn't know the anus had ever left, to tell you the truth."

Right as my mother is saying this, and totally fated, my father walks into the kitchen. My mother goes, "Michael, did you know the anus is back?"

My father looks at my mother and shakes his head.

I go, "Pa, Mommy doesn't know what a rim job is."

My father, in his typical deadpan way, without missing a beat goes, "I'll show her later."

And then he starts cracking up.

This, in sum, is my relationship with my parents as well as a sample—dare I say taste—of what's to come.

Part I

Part 1

1

THE BEGINNING OF THE END

Once upon a time in 1975, in the same hospital where Beyoncé would squeeze Blue Ivy out of her vagina, a small Jewess was born on the Upper East Side of the island of Manhattan. Instead of being born into rap royalty, she was born to Eve and Michael Aschenbrand. Eve was the daughter of Holocaust survivors. Eve's father had been an important journalist and Zionist who, rumor had it, worked for the Mossad or the CIA. They moved from Israel to America when Eve and her sister, Sara, were preteens. Michael was the eldest of three sons and had grown up in the East Village when it was filled with drug addicts and prostitutes. His father was a traveling salesman and his mother, a teacher. Eve and Michael named their first child Periel, which translates from Hebrew to mean "fruit of God."

In her own words, for the first time, this is the story of the first three and a half decades of her life.

Apparently, from the moment I was born three weeks early, I behaved like a small, entitled beast. My mother says that every time she put me down, I started screaming. She says that as I got older I was so mischievous she couldn't take her eyes off me for even one second. When I was about nine months old and supposed to be asleep in my crib, she heard me giggling. When she walked in and turned on the lights, she discovered me upright and screeching, delighted by my Pollockesque accomplishment of smearing feces all over the wall.

When I was around two and a half, my mother had a horrible toothache and urgently needed to go to the dentist. Because my father was abroad for work and it was so last-minute, she called her younger sister, Sara, who at the time was in her twenties. My aunt, who was single and living the high life in downtown New York City, agreed to watch me but had no idea what to do with a two-year-old.

My aunt didn't have kids, didn't want kids, and quite frankly didn't like them very much. Sara had left home at seventeen and by the time this request came in, she was twenty-six years old and had already been married and divorced twice. She spent her time partying and fornicating—not taking care of toddlers.

My mother told her to put me in my stroller and take me for a walk and I would probably fall asleep. So my aunt, having no clue what to do with me, pushed me all the way from her apartment on Ninth Street to Thirty-Fourth Street. She said that I did indeed fall asleep on the walk, but that by the time we got to Thirty-Fourth Street, I was wide awake. Panicked I would start screaming if I was left unstimulated, she took me inside a grocery store just to keep me entertained. She wheeled me around the aisles and started to notice that people were staring at us. She couldn't figure out why until she finally looked down at me and saw that I had removed my diaper, had both of my legs up in the air, and was masturbating wildly.

My aunt: "I never wanted to have kids to begin with, but if there was ever any doubt, that cemented it. And to make matters worse, when we got home, I realized that not only had you taken the liberty to pleasure yourself in the supermarket, but you had also stolen a bottle of shampoo!"

My aunt, who is never embarrassed by anything, wanted to die of humiliation. My mother, who is the most prim and proper person on the planet, was totally nonplussed. According to her, this behavior was typical. And it got worse.

By three years of age, as long as I was indoors, I refused to wear clothing, with the exception of my mother's red rubber kitchen gloves, which I would put on my feet and run around the house in, pretending to be a chicken. At four years old, on a class trip to the zoo, I tried to climb into the penguin cage. At six, pretending to be Mary Lou Retton, I turned my parents' bedroom into a gymnastics studio and my mother found me swinging from the canopy above their bed. She walked in right as I pulled the entire canopy out of the wall. When I was seven, I found a cockroach in the bathroom, and I quickly transformed into an exterminator, complete with ski goggles. I emptied an entire can of Lysol in the bathroom and then sealed the door with duct tape and left the roach to die. When Madonna's "Like a Virgin" came out, I was ten years old and all bets were off. I would only wear lace and lingerie and thousands of necklaces and black rubber bracelets and would not leave the house without drawing a mole on my face. Whenever we had company, I insisted on performing my Madonna routine and even took to drawing hair under my arms with my mother's eyeliner.

There was, apparently, no controlling me. My mother once told me, "I was petrified something terrible was going to happen to you because you had absolutely no fear. And you would never take no for an answer. If I said no to something, you would look up at me with your fuzzy head and your big green eyes and say, 'You doubt it, Mommy?' and I would finally just say, 'Yes, Peri, yes, I doubt it.'"

She says that she never had a second child because she was afraid to have another one "like me."

Looking back, I was extremely lucky. If I had a kid like that, I would probably have given her up for adoption, but my parents were wonderful and they adored me. We weren't rich, but we certainly were well off. My father is a native New Yorker and my mother grew up in Europe and Israel and she has very European sensibilities and it was very important to her to infiltrate my brain with culture. She started taking me to Lincoln Center and the Museum of Modern Art before I could talk.

By the time I was sixteen, I had inherited my street smarts from my father and a sense of worldliness from my mother. We had traveled widely, but beyond that, because I grew up in New York, I had been exposed to all walks of life at a very early age.

This is only to say that I figured out pretty early on that the world was a fascinating place and I wanted to see it all. I didn't think anyone owed me anything, but I knew it was my life and it would be what I made of it.

Most important, I was comfortable in my own skin. I actually *liked* myself. At sixteen, I had my first really serious boyfriend. He was great but I eventually outgrew him. Then at nineteen, I had my heart broken. And shortly thereafter, I had my first one-night stand. I quickly learned the difference between sex and love. I also learned that a guy will never like you more because you had sex with him. More important, I learned that he will never like you less, so you should pretty much do whatever the fuck you want and be yourself. And that, ladies and gentlemen, was exactly what I did.

I was twenty-two years old, living in Arizona, and finishing up my last year of college when I met Noam. Like most kids that age, I thought I knew everything. I may have been a little wise beyond my years, but not by much. But I was kind of an old soul and I did realize that life was precious and I was fascinated by the world and I knew how to enjoy myself. Noam used to say I was a good-time girl.

Noam was thirty-one when we met, which seemed old as hell back then but is five years younger than I am now. I had taken longer than usual to graduate. While everyone else was "planning for their future" I was gallivanting around the world and smoking enough pot to kill a horse. I had spent nine months in Europe and when I met Noam, I was working as a cocktail waitress in a strip club to pay it off. Noam, for his part, was getting his PhD in English literature, and while he was totally smitten with me, he found my job distasteful, to say the least.

I understood and agreed that from a feminist perspective working in a strip club was extremely problematic, but I was saving money to travel and making more in one night than most of my friends made in a week. Plus, it was interesting. The strip club was frequented by Mexican kingpin drug lords. Guys with teardrop tattoos under their eyes, with names like El Chapon used to sit around drinking Tequila Rose and call me La Flaca.

I tried to explain to Noam that the way I saw it, I was being given hundred-dollar bills to bring people napkins and that was far better than working in a smoothie bar, mashing wheatgrass for seven dollars an hour. Noam, who was far more of an intellect than I, saw little humor in all this.

Noam, by all accounts, was a sophisticated New Yorker but he was mixed with cowboy. He chose his words carefully and when he drank whiskey, he had a southern drawl. The juxtaposition of all this was irresistible. Noam was nine in 1975, the year I was born, when his mother decided they were moving from the South to New York City. They were poor hippies and they lived in raw lofts in industrial SoHo, before it was an outdoor mall crawling with tourists. His mother was working and his biological father bailed when he was a baby and Noam was left to his own devices. While I was still in diapers, he was playing his guitar on Prince Street for money. He was shy, but people were drawn to him because he was talented and gentle and beautiful in a very striking way. He was tall and lithe and had a square jaw, a perfect nose, light-brown hair, and green eyes. He eventually graduated from high school and moved to Los Angeles, where he was "discovered." There he started modeling and acting, and although he hated it and thought it was vapid and insipid, after two years he had saved enough money to transfer from community college to an Ivy League school.

Noam was fascinating and brilliant in a way I had never experienced before. By the time I met him, he was getting his PhD in literature and could quote Melville, Twain, and Shakespeare. He looked like a model (which he had been), but he spoke like a philosopher. He was shy but he drove a motorcycle. He was modest. And humble. And kind. And sensitive. And really funny. He was just as comfortable in a room full of New York Jews as he was at his uncle's racetrack in Oklahoma.

I'd been eyeing Noam at the gym for a couple of months before he got up the nerve to talk to me. When we finally went out on our first date, he took me to a Mexican restaurant in the heart of Tucson's barrio. After two drinks, he told me he was married.

"That's really interesting," I said, as I choked on my margarita. "And your *wife* doesn't mind that you're out on a date?"

Noam laughed and explained that he had gotten married only so his "wife" could stay in the country. Anyway, he explained, marriage was nothing more than social and legal construct. My eyes nearly popped out of my head as everything I had been taught about marriage went straight out the window. This was the most reasonable thing I had ever heard and yet, so *shocking*. Meeting Noam made me realize that I had grown up in the most traditional household in the world. I had always thought I was radical. Noam actually *was* radical. It was easy to be exceptionally daring, brimming with self-confidence, and afraid of nothing when you had a safety net.

And it's not that I was sheltered. I wasn't. I had the street smarts of a kid who grew up in Queens but I had lofty aspirations. I knew from a very young age that I was in the wrong borough. At seventeen, I moved west to attend university and swore to myself I would make something interesting of my life if it was the last thing I ever did. I did not want to spend my life living on Queens Boulevard. And all it took was one glance around to discern that most of the people there would never get out. Most of the people I grew up with live on the same block they did twenty years ago.

I liked Tucson because although there was no water to speak of, the climate reminded me of Israel, where I had spent a considerable amount of time as a child with my mother's family. I fantasized that I would eventually move back to New York City to live a glamorous life and do something artsy, and I imagined that at some point I would poison my father's parents and take over what was rightfully mine—the giant two-bedroom apartment my father grew up in.

Noam, having grown up in a more bohemian time, was less enamored with this lifestyle than I was. He loathed what Manhattan had become. And although he was a gentile, he understood the neuroses of a Jewish girl from New York even if he didn't share them, which made for a good balance. He was wonderful but he also suffered from depression, the way people who so deeply understand the world can. It was a difficult thing for me to understand at such a young age. Being older and having experienced more than I, Noam was also more hardened. He loved that I was optimistic but he was a pessimist by nature. Early in our relationship, when I told him I'd love him unconditionally, he matter-of-factly said, "P, nothing is unconditional."

I naïvely thought that if I just loved him enough, everything would be okay. And I did love him. I knew that because of him I was becoming a smarter and more interesting person. He taught me that things were complicated and nuanced. He taught me to be less reactionary. To live a life with Noam meant that there was a way to live that really wasn't within the cookie-cutter confines of how most people lived. And I valued this.

But I was young. After about six or so months together, I cheated on him. When I finally got up the courage to tell him that I had had sex—and with a girl, no less—he barely flinched. He understood my desire to experience the world. He was a wise, wonderful, understanding person who granted me the freedom and the support to do anything and everything I ever wanted or needed to do. He understood that I was young and needed to experience life and he wasn't petty or judgmental. Being with him was the best of both worlds.

When I finally graduated from college, I got offered a job that would send me to Thailand for a year. We never discussed sex with other people or the boundaries of our relationship.

While I was there, we spoke on the phone and wrote long letters and e-mailed, and halfway through my stay Noam visited. We had missed each other and it was clear that when I came back, we'd be together again.

But when he left, I had a brief affair with a really hot Israeli medic on a weeklong rafting trip in Nepal. I hadn't had sex with anyone *before* Noam visited, so it was strange that I did after he left but for some reason it seemed okay to me. I traipsed around India for a while and eventually, after about a year away, I made my way back to Arizona for graduate school. I never mentioned my fling, he never asked, and I just pretended nothing ever happened. It was entirely possible that Noam had indiscretions of his own in my absence but it was a subject neither one of us ever broached.

We were happy to be reunited and that was enough. Shortly thereafter, we found a beautiful rammed-earth house and moved in together, probably too quickly. Then we got a dog. I named him Eli, after the Jewish prophet Elijah, because he turned up on our doorstep during Passover dinner. It was, by all accounts, domestic bliss. But it was also absurd. As much as I loved Noam, to think that someone like me would be ready to settle down in her early twenties was outrageous. And even though neither one of us ever said it, we both knew it. This became a very problematic theme in our relationship: instead of dealing with our issues, we just pretended they didn't exist.

Two years later I finished graduate school and reality set in. And that was when things got complicated. I was twenty-six and ready for another adventure. Noam was thirty-five and ready to settle down. I was antsy. Among other things, our sex life had taken a turn for the worse; i.e., it was nonexistent. I, who wanted to have sex every minute of every day since I discovered

I had a clitoris, was beside myself. Instead of actually dealing with it, I decided to go away again, this time to Paris for the summer. I had no idea what I was going to do when I got back, so we got rid of our house. I went to Paris and tried to figure out what it meant to be a writer. Part of what this entailed was having an affair with a butch lesbian and a really hot artist with the most enormous penis I had ever seen and who looked exactly like Jean-Michel Basquiat.

So I went to Europe for the summer and Noam stayed in Tucson. He decided that after the summer he would move back to New York, and he wanted me to come with him. I had decided that I could not yet move to New York because I needed to move to Los Angeles. Instead of breaking up, we decided to have a long-distance relationship. And somehow this all seemed very reasonable. In the interim, indeed, the day after I arrived from Paris, I received a phone call at the crack of dawn.

I don't do anything well at six o'clock in the morning except sleep. And I couldn't imagine what my mother wanted from my life at six AM. I assumed she had forgotten that since she was in New York and I was in Arizona that there was a three-hour time difference.

The second I heard her voice, I knew something horrible had happened.

I was right.

My mother told me that two planes had just flown into the Twin Towers. Moreover, my friend Lori's older brother, Guy, was nowhere to be found. Lori and I had been best friends since we were thirteen. I slept at her house nearly every weekend and had a huge crush on Guy all through high school. I hadn't spoken to her in a few years. We had had some big dumb fight but I called her anyway. I figured the worst she could do was hang up on me, which thankfully she didn't. I actually caught her as she was on her way to Guy's apartment to pick up his toothbrush so the authorities would have something with his DNA so they could identify his body—if they ever found it. Lori told me that she and Guy didn't speak on the phone very often but for some reason, the previous night she had spoken to him for two hours. Seemingly out of nowhere, Guy told her that he was sick of his job at Cantor Fitzgerald and was going to quit soon and pursue his true love—music. He had been thinking about it for a long time, he said, and he was ready to make his move.

The next day was September 11, 2001.

This story would resonate with me for the next decade.

Noam did move to New York and I did move to Los Angeles. I started a T-shirt company and I wrote a book and I had more affairs. It was a very productive few years but my relationship with Noam was on precarious ground. I mean, obviously. I'd been hemming and hawing for years and he finally gave me an ultimatum: come to New York or it was over for good. I decided to move and it was fair enough on his end, but in hindsight, if you have to give someone an ultimatum, that's never a good sign. And though we really, truly loved each other, we ultimately were more best friends than anything else.

All in all, we were together for more than ten years. It seemed possible that for as much as we loved each other, the things we loved about each other in the beginning were the things that would tear us apart. When our lease was finally up in our Nolita sublet, Noam was dead set on moving to Brooklyn and I was dead set on staying in Manhattan. His bohemian nature and my bourgeois tendencies were clashing. Big-time. Noam wanted to teach English in a disenfranchised neighborhood in Brooklyn. He wanted to give underprivileged kids a chance at a great education; he wanted a simple life.

I, perhaps more than ever, still wanted everything I had escaped Queens in search of—like Chanel bags. And maybe it's not exactly that I escaped Queens in search of Chanel bags—as there are more Russian ladies than you can count who have Chanel bags and live in Queens. But I did escape in order to find something . . . *grander*. And Noam just wasn't interested in those things. So our lives became very separate. I wasn't particularly crazy about his friends, and he wasn't particularly crazy about mine. We rarely went out together because we didn't enjoy doing the same things. And if we did, I wanted to take taxis and he wanted to take the subway. We were constantly butting heads.

The last thing in the world I wanted to do was move to Brooklyn. As far as I was concerned, I hadn't clawed my way out of one outer borough to move to another. I knew all about how great Brooklyn was and how cool it had become and how beautiful it was and everyone we knew who lived there loved it. As far as I was concerned, in spite of all that, there was still one fundamental problem with Brooklyn: it wasn't Manhattan.

I knew from the first time I went to the Patricia Field store in the Village (back when it was on Eighth Street) when I was thirteen and watched the queens getting ready to go out at night that I was living in the wrong borough. It was painfully clear that everything was much more exciting on the other side of the bridge. I didn't want to *see* the skyline; I wanted to *live* in it.

By the end, before we moved out, we had pretty much stopped having sex altogether, which helped me rationalize the fact that I was cheating on Noam nearly every opportunity I got. And it all *seemed* fine in some fucked-up way since we had *still* never, ever in all of our more than ten years together had a conversation about this. It was almost a silent agreement that what we didn't know couldn't hurt us. And there was just so much that was unsaid.

Euripides said, "A slave is he who cannot speak his thoughts." And in that relationship, for whatever reason—for *many reasons*— I could not speak my mind. Mostly, I think, I wasn't speaking because to speak would have been to acknowledge the painful fact that we were like two pieces of a puzzle that simply did not fit. And I knew that. We both did.

We were still living together when I shot the pilot for my first book, but I knew it was the beginning of the end. The whole experience was thrilling for me and I became more self-consumed than ever.

Because it was everything I had been dreaming of, it was the perfect excuse to not deal with my relationship. In my megalomaniacal frenzy, I had somehow convinced my agent to convince the producer to let me "act" as "myself." This was the stupidest idea I had ever had, primarily because I know nothing about acting and shy of a minor role in *Oliver Twist* when I was nine, I had never so much as even been on a stage. But minor details like these have never prohibited me from following my dreams. It's likely that this is also why the pilot never got picked up.

My brief stint on the fringe of Hollywood gave me a whole new understanding for on-screen romances. At first I was kind of skeptical, but after being naked together for three days, my "love interest" was actually starting to turn me on. I was not only convinced that I was on my way to superstardom, but I was also convinced that Seth and I had real chemistry. I had reconciled the fact that getting naked and making out with

Seth was "acting." And Noam never even *asked* me what we were shooting, so as usual I just kept my mouth shut.

One day after we wrapped, as they say in the industry, I leaned in to kiss Seth, which we had done a hundred times already. But Seth pulled away from me and said no.

I was baffled, to say the least. "Excuse me?"

Seth said, "Periel, you have a boyfriend."

I was genuinely perplexed. I was like, "Yeah? And?"

And Seth said, "*And* you live with him."

I said, "And?"

Seth was like, "Periel, I don't hook up with girls who have boyfriends."

I couldn't believe what a philistine he was!

I was like, "Seth, it's a little bit more complicated than that."

And Seth goes, "Maybe for you it is. For me, it's not complicated at all."

And, implementing what I had learned from Noam, I said, "Seth, things are not black-and-white."

Seth said, "Maybe for you they're not. That's *your* shit. My shit is that you have a boyfriend and I don't hook up with girls who have boyfriends."

Buddha says that you should learn from experiences like these and be grateful to have a bruised ego. And really, who better to take advice from than Buddha? So while in the short term I was mortified, in the long term I think I did learn a thing or two. For example, if you are trying to have sex with someone while you are in a relationship with someone else, it's pretty likely that something is seriously wrong with your relationship. If you're trying to have sex with someone while you're in a relationship with someone else, instead of focusing your attention on trying to get laid, you should focus your attention on being honest with yourself as to *why* you're in that relationship to begin with.

In those moments when I was not distracting myself, I knew in my bones that everything was far from okay. I eventually came to terms with the fact that, ultimately, it's yourself you have to face every morning in the mirror, so you damn well better like what you see. This was becoming more and more difficult.

When there were only weeks left to move out and find a new apartment and we hadn't, I found myself, literally, on my knees in the bathroom, with my head in my hands, knowing that if we didn't end it now, I was going to wake up in five years and be in the exact same place I was right then. And I would never forgive myself.

Noam eventually did move to Brooklyn and I moved into my friend Hanna's apartment down the block. After ten years, we had broken up for real and it was the most painful thing I had ever done. I can't remember ever having felt more sad or empty inside. It felt like part of me was missing and there was nothing I could ever do it to get it back.

2

LOSER IN LOVE

It was incredibly kind of my friend Hanna to take me in after Noam and I broke up so that I wouldn't be homeless. Plus, Hanna is so crazy that focusing on her dysfunction was much less traumatic than dealing with my own. Hanna is awesome—funny, talented, great-looking—but she is totally out of her fucking mind. She had always been particularly neurotic and insecure, but *especially* when it came to men. It was a testament to what a mess my life was becoming that *I* was taking advice from *her*. We'd been friends since we were thirteen and I had always been the wild and fearless one and she had been more careful and timid. While it never even occurred to me that people might be talking about me, she was always worried about what people thought. Her neuroses were as crippling as they were charming.

Her neuroses came as no great surprise given her history. Her parents were pretty out of it while we were growing up, so we used to go to her house and take over her basement with weeklong parties and no one ever noticed. But when her mom got mad at her, she used to scream and throw shoes at Hanna. In addition to throwing shoes at her, her mother also used to tell her on a regular basis that her girlfriends were no good, she should trust no one, and she had better find a nice, rich Jewish man to marry her. We were *fifteen*.

This constant badgering turned Hanna into a nervous wreck. Despite her beauty, her talent, her charm, and her wit, she was so insecure and nervous around guys that she didn't get laid until she got to college. And that experience was such a disaster that to this day the only way she can have an orgasm is by masturbating. She has literally *never* come from having sex with another person. The good news was that no matter how down I was, her stories would always cheer me up.

I would say, "Hanna, *please* tell me the story about Jonathan. It's the only thing that is going to make me feel better."

Hanna would answer, "Oh, God, Peri, not this again."

But since we were kids, she has always given in to my peer pressure and would always acquiesce. "Fine. But you better not write about it."

As I sat in front of her with a notebook and a pen and scribbled furiously, I said, "I won't, I promise."

Hanna: "I met Jonathan in college when I was eighteen years old. He was my first real boyfriend and I was a virgin."

Me: "Why were you a virgin?"

Hanna: "You know why I was a virgin! All the guys in high school were assholes and I was waiting to be in a relationship to have sex."

Me: "Was your first time as good as you'd hoped?"

Hanna: "Well, no. It wasn't exactly what I'd thought it would be."

Me: "Why not?"

Hanna: "Well, we would start to hook up and he would always stop in the middle—"

Me: "Why?"

Hanna, glaring at me: "You know why! He had erectile dysfunction."

Me: "Did he *tell* you that?"

Hanna: "He didn't have to *tell* me. It was obvious! Plus, I knew he was on Prozac and I thought that was why he couldn't keep it up. I thought it was the perfect situation. He was a really nice Jewish boy. But every time we were right about to have sex, he just couldn't get it up. Until—"

Me: "Until what?"

Hanna: "Until we realized that there was only one way he got superexcited . . ." She trailed off.

Me: "Hanna! Can you put your phone down and concentrate please."

That's the other thing about Hanna. She has the attention span of a mouse and she is *constantly* distracting herself from real life by way of her phone or her computer.

Hanna: "Okay, sorry! We figured out how he could get turned on and stay excited."

Me: "This is getting me excited."

Hanna: "It is?"

Me: "Yes. And I'd be even more excited if you continued."

Hanna: "Okay. When he introduced the topic of diapers, he became ridiculously turned on and I didn't understand why, but I was so excited by the fact that he could stay hard that I didn't even care."

Me: "How does something like that get introduced into the conversation? Hey, want to fuck? Got a diaper?"

Hanna: "I don't think we ever actually *used* diapers. We just talked about them. All I had to do was describe them and he would go insane."

Me: "Is that true?"

Hanna: "Yes."

Me: "I thought you told me you *did* use them."

Hanna: "Well, I never wore one."

Me: "I know *you* never wore one. I thought *he* wore one."

Hanna: "I really don't remember. I don't think so."

Me: "Hmmmm."

Hanna: "Does that make the story worse?"

Me: "Yes. No. I don't know. It doesn't matter. Just go on. So what would you say?"

Hanna: "What?"

Me: "To him."

Hanna: "About what?"

Me: "What do you mean about what? *Stop* texting! About the fucking weather."

Hanna: "About the weather?"

Me: "Oh my God, you are impossible. Concentrate. No! Not about the weather. About diapers!"

Hanna: "Oh, right. I would have to talk about how it smelled like baby powder and it was white and soft and cushy. Or 'I'm wearing a diaper.' Or 'You're wearing a diaper.' It was a really long time ago. I don't really remember the details but just that all I had to do was say the word 'diaper' and he would just go berserk. That was more or less the only thing I could say or do for him to actually stay hard."

Me: "That's wild."

Hanna: "No, what's wild is that is how I lost my virginity . . . On top of someone who was balding and clinically depressed, while talking about diapers."

Me: "And you really didn't think this was strange?"

Hanna: "At first I did, but in the end I just wanted to lose my virginity so that the pressure was off the next time around."

The scariest part of this was that it actually made sense.

Me: "Fair enough. Do you think this fucked you up? Do you think it's why you can't come when you have sex with men?"

Hanna, stoically: "I don't think so. I just talked about diapers. People do things that are way worse."

Me: "Can we call Jonathan?"

Hanna: "No!" Pause. "I just found out he's married." Pause. "*And* he has a baby."

Me: "He has a baby?"

Hanna: "Yes. He has a baby."

Me: "That is highly disturbing. I can just imagine his wife telling her friends, 'I really wasn't expecting it, but Jonathan is so wonderful with the baby, so helpful. He changes her diaper all the time!'"

Hanna: "I know, it's kind of scary."

Me: "He probably jerks off into the baby's diaper."

Hanna: "Peri! That's disgusting! He does not!"

Me: "These fetishes don't go away you know. You can't change what turns you on. This is actually not terribly uncommon."

Hanna: "How do you know?"

Me: "Because I've read about it. There's a whole community of these people. They are called ABDLs."

Hanna: "What is an ABDL?"

Me: "Adult baby diaper lover."

Hanna: "You're lying."

Me: "I am not lying. Look it up. I'm surprised that with the amount of time you waste on the Internet trying to find men and all the freaks you talk to that you haven't encountered one of them. Would you ever date someone now with a diaper fetish?"

Hanna, without missing a beat: "If he was hot."

This is another reason why I love Hanna. In spite of it all, she has a great sense of humor, which is a lot more than you can say about most people.

Me: "Good answer. You're pretty open-minded. I admire that about you."

Hanna: "Not really. I'm not into bondage or anything. That stuff doesn't really do it for me."

Me: "I'm not talking about bondage. I mean in general, when it comes to sex, you're pretty open-minded."

Hanna: "I don't know. Jonathan was your all-around nice, normal Jewish guy."

Yet another reason I enjoy Hanna—because she is completely delusional.

Me: "Uh, no, Hanna, he was not your all-around nice, normal Jewish guy."

Hanna: "What do you mean?"

Me: "I'm sorry to report that having a diaper fetish is not normal."

Hanna: "Well, on the surface he was normal."

Me: "On the surface Ted Bundy was normal."

Hanna: "He wasn't hurting anyone."

Me: "Ted Bundy wasn't hurting anyone?"

Hanna: "No! Jonathan wasn't hurting anyone!"

Me: "I'm not saying he was hurting anyone. People who fuck dead bodies aren't hurting anyone either, but it's still pretty kinky."

Hanna: "That's not kinky. Kinky is fun and exciting. Diapers and dead bodies are just fucked-up."

Me: "It's pretty fucked-up. I'll grant you that."

Hanna: "What's fucked-up is that is how I lost my virginity. But, honestly, I don't care anymore. I made up for it. After Jonathan, I had a one-night stand in Israel with a South African on a kibbutz because I wanted to just get it over with and be free."

Me: "How did that work out?"

Hanna: "I got a venereal infection and had to come back to the States to go to the doctor."

Me: "*What?* Are you serious? *That* really is fucked-up."

Hanna: "I know. I think God was punishing me."

Me: "That's the most ridiculous thing I've ever heard in my life. You think God was punishing you? What do you think God was punishing you *for*, exactly?"

Hanna: "Having a one-night stand? Being free-spirited in the Holy Land?"

Me: "I don't think God punishes people for that sort of thing, even if it does take place in the Holy Land. Instead of self-flagellating, it's probably better to focus on how far you've come since then."

Hanna: "How far I have come? I don't think I've come very far. That's exactly the problem."

This wasn't wholly untrue. Her past was littered with wreckage. And it's not that *all* our pasts weren't littered with wreckage, but Hanna's pile was particularly high.

Hanna: "I'm a loser in love. Oh God. Are you going to make me look like a loser in love in your book? You better not!"

I wasn't buying this whole "loser in love" thing. Hanna had shitty luck with men because she picked shitty men. Instead of figuring out *why* she picked shitty men, she just kept making one terrible decision after the next. She was like a fat person who ate doughnuts all day and then complained that they couldn't lose weight.

She was a member of every single dating website that existed—from Plenty of Fish to Jewish Singles—and she had long, extended conversations and weird intimate online interactions with men she'd never met. She also religiously visited a dating counselor, a therapist, a matchmaker, and a "healer." She had a "relationship coach" who encouraged her to "look for a boyfriend like it was her job." Moreover, she implemented every last piece of idiotic advice these people gave her. The only thing she didn't do was to apply good, practical common sense to her life. She dated guys she met online who had girlfriends; she had Internet sex with strangers; it was never ending. Then she lamented that she was a loser in love. If she was, it was entirely of her own doing, but she couldn't see that.

On the upside, she was never short on great stories, which I was constantly fascinated by. For my part, it was much easier to focus on her than to deal with the fact that my own life had completely unraveled. I distracted myself endlessly with tales of her dysfunction. And she always generously obliged.

Hanna: "I had sworn off online dating and it had been a while since I had sex and I didn't want to have sex with someone I found on Casual Encounters from Craigslist."

Me: "Holy shit, have you ever done that?"

Hanna: "Yeah, but only once."

Me: "That's fucking crazy. That is *so* fucking crazy. You have to have a death wish to do that. Haven't you ever head of serial killers?! I really can't believe people do shit like that."

Hanna: "As I was saying, I really didn't want to have sex with someone from Craigslist, so I got the idea of getting an erotic massage."

Who, in their right mind is just casually like, *Hmmmm. I'm kind of horny. Maybe I'll get an erotic massage from a stranger I meet on the Internet?* I don't consider myself a particularly conservative person but when I'm alone and want to get off, my first instinct is to throw on some porn and grab my vibrator, not *hire a male prostitute.*

Hanna, continuing: "I started to do a little research online and I came across this guy's website and he made it sound really professional and he also had all these testimonials from women from all over the city."

Me: "*Testimonials?* You actually believed that? He could have written those himself!"

Hanna: "Yeah, but there were some e-mail addresses, too, so you could contact the women in case you wanted to verify."

Me, in my usual state of extreme paranoia: "He could have *created* a bunch of fake e-mail accounts and *pretended* to be other people!"

Hanna: "I suppose so, but it seemed totally legit. I guess I could have done a little more research, but it seemed fine."

This seemed like an enormous crock of shit to me. I couldn't believe her stupidity. Her naïveté. At the same time, I was also sort of impressed by her moxie.

Hanna: "I wanted to be daring and I had nothing to do that night and I was definitely feeling a little . . . What's the word?"

Me: "Horny."

Hanna: "Right. So I sent him an e-mail to test the waters. He e-mailed me back in like two minutes and he seemed very professional. I was asking a lot of questions."

Me: "That was smart. What kinds of questions were you asking?"

Hanna: "I don't know, stuff like, 'What do you look like?'"

Me: "Are you fucking insane? You should have been asking

if he had a criminal record, not what he looked like! What dif-ference does it make what he looked like?"

Hanna: "I wanted to make sure he was attractive, which al-ways helps."

Me: "I can't believe this. And?"

Hanna: "I gave him my address and about an hour later I open the door and there is a tall, lean black man standing there! I said, 'That's not you on the website, is it!' And he said that it was! I just assumed he would be a white guy—not that I'm racist."

Me: "You are racist, actually. You always have been."

Hanna: "Well, maybe I am, but that's not the point. The photo of him on his website is black-and-white, so you couldn't really tell and I didn't want to argue with him. Then I asked him where his massage table was and he said he doesn't use a massage table. He said he does the massage on the couch or the bed and that was when I started to hyperventilate."

Me: "Why did you start to hyperventilate?"

Hanna: "Because I realized what I had done and that I couldn't get out of it, and that was when I asked him if we could just do a regular massage."

Me: "And what did he say?"

Hanna: "He said he was there to make me comfortable and I was the one who decides how far he goes."

Me: "Okay."

Hanna: "Right then and there I wanted it all. I knew I was going for it."

Me: "Why? Because you felt like you could trust him?"

Hanna: "No, I just figured if I was going to pay a hundred bucks, I may as well get something out of it."

She was a cheap racist, to boot.

Me: "This is an amazing story. Go on."

Hanna: "He wanted me to get naked right away, which made me uncomfortable but then I thought of him as a doctor, so I got on my bed."

Me: "Were you naked naked?"

Hanna: "Pretty much."

Me: "What's pretty much? Yes or no?"

Hanna: "Yes. But I put music on."

Me: "What the fuck does that have to do with anything! Putting music on makes you *not* naked?"

This story was getting more outlandish by the minute.

Hanna: "Yes, Peri! I was naked! But I didn't want to hear my thoughts so I put music on and buried my head under a pillow. He gave me a regular massage for like half an hour so by the time it turned sexual, I was really comfortable."

Me: "And then? Were you turned on?"

Hanna: "Kind of. He was definitely teasing me, going around all the areas but not going there yet and then, next thing I know, he was going there. I was on my stomach and . . . oh my God . . . maybe I *should* call him again."

Me: "Oh my God! Will you please go on!"

Hanna: "What do you want to know?"

Me: "What do you mean, *What do I want to know?* You get to the best part of the story and you ask me what I want to know? *What did he do! What happened next!*"

Hanna: "After thirty minutes of regular massage, he just started, you know . . . I can't say."

Me: "What do you mean you can't say! Have you lost your mind? You're a grown woman talking about sex! Get it together!"

Hanna: "Okay, okay! He started massaging me down there."

Me: "*Down there?* What, are you a victim of child abuse? What's *down there?*"

Hanna: "In my privates! I think he put condoms on his fingers."

I started to freak out.

Me: "I'm not going to even address the fact that you just referred to your vagina as your *privates*. He put condoms on his fingers?"

Hanna: "I told you he was professional."

Me: "I *cannot* believe he put condoms on his fingers! So he was fingering you? *Fully* fingering you?"

Hanna: "Yes. In both places."

Me: "In *both* places? No fucking way! In your butt?"

Hanna: "Yes, Peri, in my butt! That's what we're talking about, isn't it?!"

Me: "Keep going."

Hanna: "The part that's most important is that he was desperately trying to give me an orgasm and I wasn't having one."

Me: "Let me just get this straight. You are lying on your bed, naked, with an erotic masseur you found online fingering your anus, and you're thinking what, exactly, at this point?"

Hanna: "I'm thinking that he needs to lay off the butt. And I told him to stop and he never did it again. Which was a real bummer. I'm sorry I ever said anything."

Me: "So what happened next?"

Hanna: "He kept saying that he wanted to me to come. And of course, I couldn't. I asked him if all the other women come when he massages them and he said yes. He really wanted me to have an orgasm and I told him it wasn't him, that I can't orgasm with *any* guy and then we started talking about it. He seemed genuinely concerned and then he stayed in my apartment for like four hours trying to get me off and of course, it wasn't working *because I can't come!* After a while, I wasn't even horny anymore. I told him he should leave and on his way out he told me he could help me with my sexuality!"

Me: "So then what happened?"

Hanna: "The next day I called my relationship coach and signed up for ten sessions."

I started to wonder if this is what would happen to my life, too. I could deal with getting fingered by a handsome black stranger but I would kill myself if I ever wound up with a relationship coach. What Hanna needed and very likely what I needed was some good old-fashioned introspective therapy—and probably a swift kick in the ass.

3

ON MY KNEES

While Hanna was busy making a mess of her personal life and I was busy judging her, my own life was totally falling apart and I was doing everything humanly possible to ignore it. I missed Noam terribly and it had become eminently clear that we were not getting back together. Instead of getting easier, it was getting more difficult. I felt like a part of me had died and the only thing I could muster the energy to do was light my cigarettes. I felt totally unstable, like I was riding a wild bull. My safety net was gone and I was second-guessing myself in a way I had never second-guessed myself before in my life.

It's not like Noam was an asshole or had done anything terrible, and this made it harder to reconcile the breakup. Ultimately, he was a wonderful guy who adored me. Most girls would have gotten married and started having kids with him—which is precisely what Noam had wanted. Part of why we had broken up was because I knew I couldn't commit to it. And after being with him for a decade, I knew that if I still couldn't make that kind of a commitment, I probably never would.

It wasn't fair to either of us to stay together but I still felt broken and totally defeated. I started to wonder if I would feel like this forever and if I would ever find anyone who loved me like Noam had. After ten years, I was totally and abruptly unshackled. I had never been a depressed person but suddenly I didn't want to do anything but lay on the couch.

In the midst of all this, my grandmother, in perhaps the biggest favor she had ever done for me in her entire life, dropped dead. That sounds a little bit more dramatic than it actually was. It's not like she was fine and suddenly fell off a cliff. Since my grandfather died ten years earlier, her health had steadily declined. And even though she was pushing ninety I don't think anyone expected her to die. She was tough as nails and a real firecracker. Grandma was born in 1918 and she was really kind of a groundbreaker. She went to college in the 1930s when it was unheard of for women to do that sort of thing and she didn't sew or cook or clean. Nothing ever stopped her from doing anything and in a way I think we all thought she'd be around forever.

Her personality was larger than life and she said what was on her mind, no matter what. Even toward the end, while we were in the hospital, she complained that the doctors weren't doing anything to help her and that she was being starved to death. When her doctor, a lovely Japanese woman named Dr. Fujita, offered to get my grandmother a sandwich, Grandma said, "Chicken sandwich? Chicken sandwich? How about you get me some chicken chow mein!"

Dr. Fujita giggled in the way that Asian people giggle when they are embarrassed and something really isn't funny at all and quickly scurried out the room.

I was so mortified I almost crawled underneath her bed. I

was like, "Grandma! First of all, that's horrible! Second of all, Dr. Fujita is Japanese, not Chinese!"

My grandmother, who was essentially on her deathbed, said, "Your grandfather was almost killed in Pearl Harbor."

Me: "What does that have to do with anything! It's still a horrible thing to say! And since when did Grandpa serve in Pearl Harbor? I thought he was a traveling salesman!"

Grandma: "He was."

Me: "So he served in Pearl Harbor before that?"

Grandma: "Peri, don't drive me crazy with details right now. And you should really do something about your hair. I could turn you over and mop the floor with your head."

It was impossible to tell if my grandmother was just being racist as usual or if she was suffering from dementia. When Jyllian, a cousin we hadn't seen in years, stopped by, my grandmother didn't recognize her at first. After she left, Grandma spat, "Who could be surprised I didn't recognize her? She's so swollen she looks pregnant!"

While Jyllian was telling Grandma about her new boyfriend, Grandma said, "Well, he's got to be better than the last one. The last one looked like you dragged him out of the gutter."

After Jyllian left, someone mentioned it was nice of her to have stopped by, and Grandma said, "You can't make a silk purse out of sow's ear."

That, in a nutshell, was my grandmother. She was quick to judge, had a tongue like a whip, and regardless of whether you were interested, she always said exactly what she thought. She was funny and smart and the only compliments she ever gave were to herself. She could be great fun to be around, but she was super self-absorbed.

I had begged her for years to add my name on her lease so

I could one day inherit her giant, rent-controlled apartment but she categorically refused. She was worried she would be evicted, she said, which was nonsense. Even at the end of her life, when there was no risk of anything, she wouldn't do it. So while my father and his brother, who is affectionately known as Uncle Bark, were busy making funeral arrangements, I was doing what any New Yorker worth her salt would do—plotting to take over her apartment. The rest of my family was so fractured and dysfunctional no one even noticed that I had become a full-blown squatter. I thought maybe Jyllian would have the gall to show up with her hand out (which I was prepared to cut off) but she never did.

Uncle Bark, for his part, was pleased to keep the apartment in our clutches, as it was just another way to stay close to Grandma. As the youngest son, he was the baby of the family and very close to his mother. Uncle Bark is one of my favorite people in the world but he is extremely sentimental and hysterical, in every sense of the word. Uncle Bark is constantly bugging out about something totally insignificant.

For example, the first Mother's Day after Grandma died, the whole family planned to go out to a Korean barbecue restaurant for dinner. Well, Uncle Bark had a fucking meltdown. He started going on and on about his diet and his high blood pressure. And then he started screaming, "I am *not* going to a Korean restaurant so I can have a stroke from all the sodium! You can all go to the Korean restaurant and I'll go weep over my mother's grave."

So while he can be a huge pain in the ass, his bark is much worse than his bite, which is how he got his nickname. But I digress. Other than Uncle Bark and my parents, I'm not even sure anyone noticed I had moved in. Even during the week we sat shivah to mourn, I was surreptitiously hauling suitcase after suitcase into the apartment, but the errant family members were so wrapped up in their own greed that mine went unnoticed. My role as grieving granddaughter was never overshadowed by my real role as new tenant.

And just to be clear, I was tight with my grandmother. She was awesome in her own way. She wasn't a particularly warm person but I knew she loved me and I loved her, too. She taught me to stick up for myself and not to take no for answer. And even if she didn't really mean to, she taught me to follow my dreams.

I eulogized her at her funeral. And even though she would never have admitted it, I think I made her proud.

I have to start by thanking my father and Uncle Bark for setting such an incredible example. Though they can both be a real pain in my ass, I am positively humbled by the way they took care of Grandma. But to pay true homage to Grandma, this speech has to be spunky not sappy.

So here goes.

I am so my grandmother's granddaughter. From my stunning sense of style to my fabulous fashion to my good looks, I inherited all of Grandma's good points. And there were many. She was smart and sarcastic and sassy and witty and wise and she was fiery and funny and you could always count on her to tell it like it was. I've inherited that, too.

Grandma never gushed over me or showered me with compliments—not because she didn't love me but because that just wasn't her way. She showed her love in other ways. Like how when I told her I loved her, the way she would say, "And I love you, too, dear." Or just the way when I would crawl up beside her and hold her hand and she would let me. Letting you was a big deal with Grandma. With Grandma, there were no free rides. You had to earn your keep. Grandma didn't mince her words. Compliments were few and far between and that was fine because when they came, you knew she meant them. She said what she meant and she meant what she said.

Like when I would say, "Don't I look gorgeous, Grandma?" She would answer, "You get it from me, dear." And I did get it from her. I got a lot of things from her.

Many years ago, I fell down a flight of steps and hurt my back. Grandma rushed to meet me at the emergency room. They were taking forever to see me and Grandma wasn't having it. Finally, a nurse came up to me and said, "Please, we'll do whatever you want, just please keep your grandmother away from us." I can only hope that I was half as helpful when she needed me.

Anyway, it went on a bit, but that was the gist of it. After the eulogy, Uncle Bark's rabbi (who pulled up to the gravesite in a convertible red Porsche) told me that my grandmother was lucky to have had such a good-looking granddaughter, which was superclassy.

The other person who was classy was Aunt Ruth. Uncle Bark was fuming because Aunt Ruth, who didn't even like Grandma and certainly hadn't lifted a finger to help while she was alive, had actually approached him at the funeral home and literally, while standing over *Grandma's dead body,* tried to take Grandma's gold cuff off her corpse because it was "a shame to bury her with it." If that wasn't bad enough, she then asked what her cut would be.

I was like, "Listen, B, just tell her that you and I went through the will and what she's getting will probably fill a condom. So she can bend over and I'll shove it up her ass."

Uncle Bark began howling with laughter. I knew he was devastated but I also knew I could always make him laugh with a good Aunt Ruth joke. Aunt Ruth was ridiculous. She was tall and large like a man, and she wore so much mascara she looked like a drag queen. She acted and dressed like she was a sixteen-year-old prostitute. A typical outfit for Aunt Ruth was a skin-tight dresses with her tits hanging out and a Hello Kitty handbag. Just looking at her was embarrassing. Beyond that, Aunt Ruth wasn't even really an aunt; she was Uncle Bark's second cousin or something. The whole thing was ridiculous, but apparently they had some huge falling-out about ten years prior and he was *still* upset about it. Pretty much what it boiled down to was that Uncle Bark might be crazy but Aunt Ruth sucks.

What made the whole thing that much more absurd was that there wasn't even anything to divide. I mean it's not like Grandma was a fucking Vanderbilt. Beyond that, as far as I was concerned, I was the one living there and possession was nine-tenths of the law.

And anyway, Aunt Ruth and Jyllian didn't deserve anything. Ruth was a greedy, self-absorbed bitch. She didn't even offer her condolences. And the apple didn't fall from the tree. Jyllian, her illegitimate half sister, showed up at the hospital after years of being MIA and then again, out of nowhere, at the shivah—and with an entourage, to boot. We literally hadn't seen her in years. She had distanced herself from the entire family upon finding out we had Spanish roots. And when I say Spanish roots, what I mean is that a hundred some-odd years ago some random ancestor was apparently of Spanish descent. As I've understood it, she was on FamilyTree.com or something and came across this and became irate at the whole family for "hiding" this information from her. As if anybody knew. Or gave a shit. In any event, Jyllian moved to Spain and hooked up with some dude who owned a youth hostel in Madrid. When she showed up at our grandmother's house to pay a shivah call, with Felipé in tow, she was actually talking to me with a *Spanish* accent. And if it weren't bad enough that she showed up at all, there were like six other Spaniards with her.

I was running around cleaning and serving, as was Uncle Bark, while Aunt Ruth was shoveling bagels into her mouth. To watch her would be to think the woman hadn't eaten in a year and believe me, if you saw the size of her, you would know for shit sure that wasn't the case. Before she piled whitefish, tuna, lox, cream cheese, and egg salad on *one* bagel, she said, to no one in particular, "I'm *starving*."

I looked at Uncle Bark and whispered, "She doesn't look like she's starving."

He immediately started laughing uncontrollably. The great French philosopher, Henri Bergson, in *Laughter: An Essay on the Meaning of Comic*, concludes that laughter is corrective. I may have been depressed but at least I could still summon my sense of humor every now and again.

While I was trying to laugh my way out of a deep depression, Jyllian, Felipé, and their amigos sat in the corner, speaking among themselves *in Spanish* and barely even glancing at anyone else in the room. It was about ten o'clock at night and I'd been cleaning up for the better part of the past hour, trying to kick everyone out, but they didn't bat a fucking eye. They were just sitting and talking and eating and I was at the end of my rope and couldn't take it anymore. So I was finally like, "Listen up guys, I'm not running a tapas restaurant here. If you haven't noticed, I'm cleaning up. If you haven't noticed, I'm trying to close up shop here. In case you haven't noticed, people are actually *mourning* here."

And I *was* in mourning—not only over my grandmother's death, but also over my life, which was becoming a bigger shit show than ever. After I finally got everyone out, I went to bed. I woke up feeling like I had been hit by a truck and became totally consumed with dealing with the logistics of the apartment. Nightmare as this was, it was easier than dealing with my life. More depressed than ever, I spent the following days languishing about the apartment, drinking too much espresso, chain-smoking, and lying on my grandmother's fifty-year-old pink, plastic-covered couch, watching episode after episode of *Law & Order: Special Victims Unit*.

It's funny how things work out. I had been coveting this apartment for nearly my entire life. And now here I was, actually *living* in it, and I was more depressed than I ever knew possible. To say nothing of the fact that the place itself was depressing—the apartment hadn't been renovated in over half a century. My grandparents were cheap *and* had bad taste, which was reflected in everything they owned. The apartment was filled with all of my grandparents' earthly belongings, and though my grandfather had died years earlier there was still tons of his crap strewn about as well. Plus, my boxes were everywhere and I was pretty much living out of a suitcase since there was no room to put anything.

The closets were filled with thousands of plastic necklaces and hundreds of pairs of vinyl shoes. The bathroom was peach—peach tiles, peach towels, peach shower curtain, peach plastic tissue holder. My grandparents hadn't slept in the same bed in over a quarter of a century and, as such, the bedroom had two single beds in it. In an attempt to pretend my life was normal, I pushed the beds together to form some sort of fake king-size bed, which resulted in an enormous bed in the middle of the room with a giant dent down its middle.

I had fashioned the second bedroom, which had been my father's and Uncle Bark's bedroom and was brimming with heinous pictures of Aunt Ruth, Jyllian, and other family members we hadn't spoken to in years, into my office. This meant that it had thousands of pieces of paper strewn about, but more to the point it was pretty much a giant ashtray.

The living room housed the giant pink couch, which was actually very cool in a French chaise longue kind of way. The only problem was that I was too depressed to take the plastic cover off. The kitchen was beyond disgusting. Fake tile, cheap dishes, old, crusty stove, plastic containers shoved in every corner and, of course, the requisite three million packets of Sweet'N Low my grandmother had stolen from every diner she had ever been to. Never mind that she didn't even *use* Sweet'N Low.

I was trying to create a home for myself amid the chaos but there was no point in unpacking because I had no idea how long I was going to be there since I was there illegally. The apartment was in a state of chaos, and literally and figuratively everything was a mess. I was reeling. In addition to hardly eating, chain-smoking, drinking way too much espresso, I had begun to spontaneously gag. Even my own body was turning against me. I hadn't spoken to Noam in ages and I couldn't even say his name without bursting into tears.

My mother—my wonderful, dear, amazing, loving mother who I adore with every fiber of my being—was driving me crazy. I knew that she was worried sick about me and just trying to help, but she was nevertheless making me insane.

She had taken to sending me e-mails like these:

It was so nice to spend time with you yesterday (it never is enough time).

I appreciate your comments re: not speaking with food in my mouth, so you will not be offended by the following comments:

1. Your hair—you simply can't imagine how this "hairdo" destroys your appearance. I understand that you are upset and stressed but this looks ill-groomed.

2. Why wear a dinner dress with flip-flops? This looks like a resident in a nursing home who wants to look glamorous but can't wear nice shoes because she has old feet.

Okay, I will stop only because I do not want to stress you more. I am trying to help you improve by being objective.

I will not embarrass you in front of others (even though you do it to me).

And most of all I love you and care about you more than anyone.

Please take care,
Mommy

In addition to having to contend with my mother and Uncle Bark, my genius plan of moving into my grandmother's apartment and taking over her lease was not going as smoothly as I had imagined. The reality was that I was illegally squatting and it became eminently clear that if I wanted to stay there, I was going to have to get a lawyer. And fast.

I had been delusional to think I would be able to just *take* Grandma's apartment. I had no legal right to be there. In the biggest real estate sale in the history of New York, Stuyvesant Town, the complex where my grandparents had lived since its inception, which had originally been created for the working people of the city some sixty-odd years ago, had recently been purchased by Tishman Speyer for several billions of dollars. Tishman Speyer basically owns half of New York City. When they bought the complex they began a massive overhaul, billing it as "luxury living in the city." This is a crock of shit the proportions of which I can hardly begin to articulate. The complex looks better than it did when I was a kid, to be sure, and from a business perspective, not that I know jack shit about business, it seemed like a smart move. Most of the original residents were dead or dying and the moment a tenant kicked it, Tishman Speyer would swoop in, renovate, and quadruple the rent— which was precisely why they bought it.

Like most of their first residents, when my grandparents moved in they were paying fifty-some-odd dollars a month for their relatively large two-bedroom apartment.

By the time my grandmother died, her rent was around a thousand dollars. Of course everything is relative and while a thousand dollars is more than most people in the world make in a year, a thousand dollars a month is dirt fucking cheap for a two-bedroom apartment in downtown New York City. True, I had no business living there, but thousands of other people did. Tishman Speyer didn't give a shit about that. They were in the midst of trying to evict innocent elderly people and vacate as many apartments as humanly possible. They wanted to avoid, well, people like me at any and all cost.

They were like vultures and their little scheme wound up blowing up in their greedy little faces as the whole deal eventually went bankrupt. I may have had no business being there, but you can't just kick old people out of their homes. The other thing you apparently can't do is pretend you're a dead woman in order to take advantage of a rent-controlled apartment. At heart, even in my darkest moments, I must be an optimist. I really thought I had a chance.

I found an attorney, a nice fellow named Herbert Lust, of

all things, to try and help me. I told him the whole history, how my grandparents Lillian and Seymour Aschenbrand moved into apartment 4B in 1948 and my grandmother lived there until her death on September 12, 2008. I told him that my grandfather may or may not have fought in Pearl Harbor, that my grandmother was a New York City public school teacher, that my father and Uncle Bark had grown up in that apartment, and that it was only right that it be handed down to me. I even talked about how I was a struggling artist and how that should count for something. After I got through my heartfelt tale, I asked him whether he thought my writing an impassioned plea to Stuyvesant Town explaining all this would help my situation. Mr. Lust looked at me and said, "Tishman Speyer wouldn't piss on you if you were on fire."

He told me I could sue them if I wanted to and that he'd be happy to represent me but I would wind up spending tens of thousands of dollars (that I didn't have) and I would never win.

So I switched tactics. I decided to wait them out. I figured my best bet—and quite frankly my only option at that point— was to stay put until they realized I wasn't my grandmother, at which point they would kick me out. This, as it turned out, was exactly what happened. It would take them about nine months and we would eventually settle.

In the meantime, my newly found freedom felt more like prison. In the midst of my suffering, Uncle Bark decided we had to go through Grandma's stuff and decide what we were doing with everything so we didn't get stuck doing it when I suddenly received an eviction notice, which could happen at any moment. My father, who likes to keep things as simple as possible, wanted nothing to do with the apartment. He likes things done by the book and illegally squatting in a dead woman's apartment does *not* fall into that category. My dad's job was to handle all of Grandma's bills and other similar affairs, which he did meticulously. As far as he was concerned, we could have set everything else on fire and that would have been just fine with him. My mother was more concerned than ever—and she was calling me more than ever. And as a result I wanted to put my head through a pane of glass. Even though my mother came to this country from Israel fifty years ago, she still has the most ridiculous accent in the world.

Me, answering the phone at noon, having just dragged myself out of bed, with raspy voice: "Hello?"

My mother: "*Hallo?* Peri?"

Me: "Yes, Mommy."

My mother: "Oh! I didn't know it was you!"

Me, already losing patience: "Well, who else would it be! You just called my cell phone!"

My mother: "I know. That's why I was confused. It didn't sound like you. You sound terrible."

Me: "Is that what you called to tell me?"

My mother: "You sound like you've been smoking."

Me: Silent.

My mother: "*Have* you been smoking!"

I remained silent but could feel my blood pressure rising.

My mother: "So you *have* been smoking."

Me: "Mommy, now really isn't a good time for this."

My mother, starting to scream: "It's *never* a good time! That's exactly the problem! Every time I call you, it's not a good time! And then you say you're going to call me back and you never do! It's terrible! This is a terrible way to live! This is a terrible way to have a relationship! I don't want to come visit you in the cancer ward!"

Me, wanting to kill myself: "Mommy, relax. I'm not smoking." I said as I light a cigarette.

My mother: "I can *hear* you smoking! I don't know when this is going to end but it's not good! You don't know what you're doing to your lungs! And the whole apartment stinks like smoke! It's disgusting!"

Me: "Mommy, I *really* have to go, Uncle Bark is on his way over." And I hung up.

Then I walked into the peach bathroom and looked at myself in the mirror. And gagged. I couldn't bear to take a shower, so I splashed some water on my face and sniffed around. I really hoped the apartment didn't stink like smoke because Uncle Bark would have a heart attack and I didn't need some long talk from him about his high blood pressure.

Uncle Bark, in all of his grief and mourning and great enormous love for his dead mother was, much like myself, fairly delusional. While I was under the misguided impression that we would put everything into giant garbage bags, Uncle Bark wanted to keep *everything*. And when I say everything, I mean *everything*. Nothing was too insignificant and every last piece of junk had value. I would leave the room for a second and when I came back he would be fingering a red plastic beaded necklace as though it were an antique diamond Cartier.

And all of the stuff that he absolutely could not keep he wanted to sell. I was like, "Uncle Bark, let's just make a pile and call Goodwill." No, no, no, he wouldn't hear of it. He had this cockamamie idea that we were going to *sell* all this garbage. So I had to sit there with him and photograph all this shit and then list everything, item by fucking item, on Craigslist. It was a nightmare. I just about lost my patience when he was waxing poetic about Grandma's rug, which he kept referring to as a

"Persian-style" carpet. It was (a) mint green, (b) stained, and (c) made in China. I tried to explain that we were wasting our time (not that I had anything else to do) and that the resale value of garbage is quite low. He wouldn't hear of it. And because he had no idea how to take a photo, let alone upload one to a computer, I spent hours making ads like these:

- Salton Rolling Tea Cart with Hot Tray Top (doesn't work but can be rewired) $75.00

- Naugahyde Vinyl Recliner (does not fully recline) $40.00

- 2 "Persian-style" carpets (in good shape but need to be cleaned) $175.00 & $90.00

- Stuyvesant Town Kitchen Dinette Area Hardwood Table with Removable Leaf & 4 Matching Green Seated Chairs (minor nicks in table and chairs can be repaired) $350.00 for set

- Metal Closet with Hanging Rod & Sliding Doors (doors need to be replaced) $40.00

- Microwave (works well but needs good cleaning!) $75.00

And this was how I pretty much lived the next nine months—grieving, cleaning, or, for one reason or another, spending a significant amount of time on my knees.

4

INNOCENT UNTIL PROVEN GUILTY

On one of his many visits, Uncle Bark took one look at my tobacco-stained teeth and said, "First of all, I know you're smoking in here and it's disgusting. Second of all, you better go get your teeth cleaned. They're disgusting, too."

When Uncle Bark left, I went back into the peach-tiled bathroom and inspected the brown enamel in my mouth. I couldn't imagine garnering the energy to pick up the phone to make an appointment, let alone carry out an actual trip to the dentist's office, but I was even grossing myself out. Under the best of circumstances I loathed going to the dentist. I blamed this on my mother for forcing me to go to her freak-show dentist, Dr. Bogdanovich, when I was a kid. Dr. Bogdanovich worked out of his basement in Queens, wore a hairpiece, smelled like salami, and had bad teeth. What kind of self-respecting dentist had bad teeth? Even as a kid, I knew it was unconscionable. It was like having a fat trainer. As I was debating whether I had it in me to make it all happen, the phone rang.

Who was it? My mother. Who else would it be?

Me: "Hello."

My mother: "Hi, Pootsilé."

Pootsilé is my mother's nickname for me. It is pronounced poot-see-leh. Once when Hanna was over for dinner, she heard my mother say this and she pulled me aside and in a very concerned voice, asked, "Why does your mother call you Pussylips?!"

Me: "Hi, Mommy."

My mother: "What are you doing?"

Me: "I'm thinking about going to the dentist."

My mother: "Oh good, because you really do need to get your teeth cleaned again. I didn't want to say anything but your teeth are disgusting from all the smoking. It's really terrible. You *have to stop smoking*. I'm not kidding."

My mother is famous for saying "I didn't want to say anything, but . . ." and then she says the rudest thing in the world *and* she acts like she's doing me a favor. She also never skips a beat.

My mother: "If you want to go to Dr. Bogdanovich, he would be happy to see you again. He asks about you every time I see him. He's such a nice man."

Me: "Mommy, just because he asks about me every time he sees you does not make him a nice man!"

My mother: "He takes very good care of me and Papa. *And* takes our insurance, which is more than I can say for your dentist."

Me: "First of all, you only like Dr. Bogdanovich because he's Jewish. Second of all, I'm not even convinced that he actually *is* a dentist. Have you ever seen any evidence of this? He is a Russian immigrant with rotten teeth and a toupee who works out of his basement in Queens. That he happens to own dental equipment does not necessarily mean he is a dentist."

My mother, completely ballistic: "Okay, Peri! You know everything as usual! That is the most ridiculous thing I have ever heard in my life! And he does not work out of a *basement*! He works out of a very nice office and it just happens to be in the lower level of his home!"

Me: "Well, last time I checked, the 'lower level of a home' is actually the dictionary *definition* of the word 'basement.' And to boot, his breath always smells like salami."

My mother: "Oh, please, Peri, you are acting like a child! He's a very good dentist and he does *not* smell like salami. That's ridiculous! He may have smelled like garlic on one occasion because he had just eaten lunch."

Me: "Well, that's an unacceptable explanation. Dentists should smell like Listerine. *All the time.* And I don't know why you give a shit what dentist I go to anyway. Or why you care whether he takes my insurance. I finally found a dentist I like. Isn't that enough? And I love Leslie, my hygienist. What difference does it make to you! I mean, really!"

My mother: "Oh! I forgot how wealthy you are and that you can afford to go to a dentist on Park Avenue! And what does that mean, you *love* your hygienist? That's ridiculous! What is she, your friend?"

Me: "Well, actually, if you must know, she is kind of my friend! She's very nice and she's very gentle *and* she loved my book!"

My mother: "Oh, Peri, please! That is *not* why you pick a doctor. I really don't know what's wrong with you. What are you going to do?" My mother started screaming, "What are you going to do with your life! Do you even have a plan? You better start getting serious!"

Me: "Last time I checked I was dead serious about my life. I'm hanging up now."

Our conversation enraged me enough to call Dr. Mulligatani's office and make an appointment for a checkup *and* to have my teeth cleaned. I knew that at least everyone in the office would be nice to me. And I really did like Dr. Mulligatani. He was lovely and soft-spoken and very clean and he was always meticulously dressed. He had great teeth; beautiful, thick, slicked-back jet-black hair; a wonderful Indian accent; beautiful skin; and deep, soulful brown eyes. The first time he examined me he took one look inside my decaying mouth and determined that I had not one but *four* cavities that according to him needed to be attended to immediately. He filled two of them on the spot and told me to make another appointment for next week.

I told him I wasn't sure I was prepared for this kind of a commitment, that it was nothing personal but that I really kind of hated going to the dentist.

With a Gandhi-like calmness and a matching accent, he said, "You are in-b-iting root cah-nal. You will be bock."

I liked him, too, because he had good judgment. He knew how crazy I was, so before Dr. Mulligatani ever put anything in my mouth, he attached a mask filled with nitrous to my face. And so I trusted him. Unlike my mother, who thinks that being Jewish is the single good criteria to determine whether or not you are a good doctor, I actually need to *love* my doctors. I also need to feel like they love me.

Let me be clear here. Doctors are fucking shady. They're just as shady, if not *more* shady than everybody else. Having a degree in medicine does not qualify you to be a good doctor and it sure as shit doesn't qualify you to be a good person. I judge doctors the same way I judge everyone else—with my instincts and by observing the way they behave. Being Jewish can help, but on its own, it's not enough to cut the mustard.

As I relayed to my mother, one Dr. Allan Zarkin, a *Jewish* ob-gyn had actually *carved his initials* into a patient's abdomen after delivering her baby via caesarean. According to the *New York Times*, "Immaculately dressed in a cashmere turtleneck, Ferragamo loafers and a brown suit, the silver-haired obstetrician calmly pleaded guilty to second-degree assault. When asked by Justice White what he had done, Dr. Zarkin responded in a steady, almost soothing tone, 'Using the scalpel, I scratched my initials into her.'"

I told my mother that the state also cited the clinic where Dr. Zarkin worked "for not thoroughly checking Dr. Zarkin's credentials" and for allowing him to perform surgery unsupervised even though a psychiatrist had told clinic officials that Dr. Zarkin had a "brain disorder."

My mother said, "Maybe *you* have a brain disorder. You find a random Indian man you know nothing about and suddenly you're acting like you've discovered the best dentist in the tristate area! Your behavior is erratic and you pick your doctors for all the wrong reasons! Because they're nice? What kind of criteria is that? I'm getting very worried about the decisions you're making."

Maybe I should have been worried about certain decisions I was making, too, but going to see Dr. Mulligatani was not one of them. He was wonderful. I called Veronica, the receptionist, with whom I had also become very friendly, and made an appointment for the very next day.

In addition to the fact that my teeth were brown, I could tell they needed to be cleaned because it felt like I had a small sweater on each of them. I also knew that Leslie wouldn't judge me, that my teeth would be as good as new, and that I really had nothing to worry about as far as pain. Leslie was the gentlest hygienist I had ever met. She always took her time with my decrepit teeth, slowly bringing them back from brown to light yellow. She was always happy to see me and from the first time I met her she became my favorite hygienist in the entire world. She would tell me stories about her travels and even about her son, Dino, who was studying abroad in London. She also had the most incredible teeth I had ever seen in my life. They were so bright they almost shone. And they weren't those fake horse teeth veneers either.

I felt like I had actually accomplished something by making the appointment. And I was actually looking forward to going there. I was as excited to see Veronica as I was to see Leslie. Veronica was a fierce Puerto Rican woman and she was the one who always called me to remind me of my appointment and I appreciated that. When I got there, though, Veronica seemed quieter than usual. She said "Hey, Mami," and gave me a hug, but she was lacking her usual enthusiasm.

I didn't really think anything of it and settled in with a copy of *Better Homes and Gardens.*

As I was sitting in the dentist chair waiting for Leslie and my nitrous, a strange-looking woman walked in. Even though she was as white skinned as me, I could tell she was Latina because her eyebrows looked like they had been drawn in with a Sharpie. Having grown up in Queens, I knew this is a look that was pretty much specifically reserved for members of the Latina community. She smiled at me. Her teeth weren't great and I figured she was the cleaning lady or something. So imagine my surprise when she said, "Hi! I'm Marabelle. I'm the dental hygienist and I'll be cleaning your teeth today!"

I started to freak out and blurted, "Where's Leslie?"

Marabelle had no idea what I was talking about or who Leslie was. That made me freak out even more and I got all weird and skittish. I was like, "Well, where's the nitrous? I don't get my teeth cleaned without nitrous."

Marabelle: "Ohhhhhh, we can't use nitrous."

Me, apoplectic: "Why not!"

Marabelle: "I'm trying to get pregnant and it's really bad for the baby."

Baby? What baby? If you're *trying* to get pregnant there is no baby. That's number one. Number two, I don't know who this woman thought she was kidding. Maybe if she swallowed an in vitro clinic she would get pregnant. She looked about forty-five years old.

Me: "I don't think so." And I stood up.

Marabelle: "Is everything okay?"

Me: "No, everything is not okay."

Like a lunatic, I marched into reception and was like, "Veronica, what the fuck?"

Veronica, nonplussed: "What's the matter, Mami?"

Me: "This isn't the Puerto Rican Day parade. Cut the 'Mami' shit. Where is Leslie? And who's the *chola* with the eyebrows in there?"

Veronica sucked her teeth at me. She was like, "Mami, please, I'm the only *chola* up in this bitch. And don't worry, Marabelle will do a very good job."

I could tell that Veronica didn't like Marabelle any more than I did. I was like, "Marabelle will *not* do a very good job because Marabelle is not coming anywhere near me. You know Leslie is the only one allowed inside my mouth. Where is she?"

Veronica: "She ain't here."

Me: "I can see that, Veronica. I can see that she's not here. I can also see that I schlepped all the way to Ninety-Sixth Street, which is about eighty blocks farther uptown than I like to be, to *see* Leslie. So if she wasn't going to be here, why didn't you tell me I had to reschedule?"

Veronica, lowering her voice: "Listen, Mami. I gots to tell you something. Leslie don't work here no more."

Me, confused: "She only works at your other location?"

Veronica: "No, Mami, you not gettin' it. Leslie don't work for the company no more."

Me: "What do you mean Leslie don't work for the company no more! What happened?"

Veronica, narrowing her large Puerto Rican doe eyes into small slits: "I can't tell you . . . but . . . something—"

Me: "Something? What!"

Veronica: "Something . . . *huge*."

I start to wonder what could possibly be *so* huge. Leslie was a middle-aged Jewish woman. She shared intimate details of her life with me. For example, I knew she was a widow and currently had a new boyfriend, who worked in finance. What could be so *huge*? Whatever it was, was much less important than the fact that I needed her to clean my teeth.

I was like, "I don't want anyone but Leslie to clean my teeth."

Veronica narrowed her eyes back to slits. She was like, "What you sayin'? You don't want to be a patient here no more?"

I narrowed *my* eyes to slits. I grew up in a pretty gritty neighborhood in Queens. I'm accustomed to dealing with tough Latina bitches and was not intimidated by Veronica's nonsense. When I was fifteen, I earned my stripes (and still have scars) from a brawl with a five-foot-eight girl named Manilla. She confronted me after hearing that I called her a whore, which she was, and punched me in the face. I proceeded to beat her about the head with my wooden clog.

All of this is only to say that Veronica's tough girl act may have intimidated some people, but even in my fragile state I was unfazed. In fact, the only thing that Veronica's reluctance to tell me what happened to Leslie did was to make me more curious than ever. Veronica could tell that I was less than impressed and tried to change her tune. She was like, "Listen, Mami, I know you love Leslie and to tell you the truth, I ain't all that crazy about Marabelle myself, but she's a good hygienist. Will you at least give her a try?"

Me: "Okay, fine. But you *have* to tell me what happened to Leslie."

Veronica, lowering her voice again and getting really serious: "For real. I can't. I'll get fired."

Now I was *dying* to know what was going on. I figured if I pressed Veronica hard enough, she would probably fold, but I didn't really want to put her in that position. I decided to cut my losses for the moment. My teeth felt like they were covered in fur and I was already there, so I let Marabelle clean them, *without* nitrous so that her nonexistent fetus wouldn't be born with a third head. I bade farewell to Veronica and went home.

By the time I got there, I was seething. I hated Marabelle. She was a bitch *and* a shitty hygienist. *And* she spent fifteen minutes lecturing me about smoking and too much caffeine and all the other reasons my teeth were brown. I was like, "I know *why* my teeth are brown. I'm not here for an analysis. Your job is to clean my teeth not fucking lecture me about them."

I was sitting at my desk thinking, *Why do I care if Veronica gets fired?* I looked around the room and figured I needed a cleaning lady anyway and that maybe I could offer her a job. I was sure that she was at least as qualified as Marlene, my current cleaning lady, who had recently informed me she was taking a six-week hiatus to get a tummy tuck. First of all, who had ever heard of a cleaning lady getting plastic surgery? Second of all, she was obviously being grossly overpaid if she could afford to get twenty thousand dollars' worth of elective surgery. But now was not the time to think about Marlene turning herself into Joan Rivers. Now was the time to put to good use my investigative FBI skills and the knowledge I had gained from watching criminal investigations on *Law & Order*.

As I stared into the blank computer screen, I wondered how I would ever get to the bottom of this and find out what happened to Leslie. I decided Veronica getting fired would be a small sacrifice in the grand scheme of things. Suddenly it hit me. It was so fucking obvious but it took me more than half an hour of sitting in front of my computer to figure it out.

I typed LESLIE MYRON into Google.

I was so shocked that I honestly, quite literally, almost fell out of my chair. The first thing that came up was a headline from the *New York Times* from a few years back that read, "Simple to Solve Slaying Is Neither Simple nor Solved."

The story is as follows:

A businessman, named Mervin Myron, was found slain in his office. He had been stabbed, *twenty-seven times* in the back, neck and chest. According to the article:

Neither Mr. Myron's wallet nor the five hundred dollars inside was taken, so burglary was ruled out. He was apparently killed shortly after the security guard's normal quitting time, a telltale sign that the killer might have been acquainted with the victim's schedule and routines . . . in the kind of brutal attack that usually points the police toward a drug user, a person with a history of mental illness or someone closely related to the victim.

The *Times* article went on to explain that his widow, *Leslie Myron*, a health care professional, was now embroiled in an intense battle with the life insurance company from which she was attempting to collect *two million dollars*. And while she had never actually been charged with his murder, she was very much a person of interest.

And, from the *Daily News*:

The owner of a major Manhattan business was found stabbed to death in his office in a murder that had police stymied yesterday. The victim was identified as Mervin Myron, owner of MGT Inc., a $20-million-a-year, 100-employee company.

Myron was last seen alive late Thursday by the last employee who left the office. His body, lying in a large pool of blood, was found there by another employee Friday at 5:45 a.m., said Detective Ed Murphy. Robbery did not appear to be the motive, detectives said. The office wasn't in disarray, and his gold-and-silver Rolex was on his wrist. He had been stabbed numerous times, police said.

I couldn't believe it. I was totally floored. *Could it possibly be my Leslie?*, I asked myself. Then I asked myself, *Are you a fucking moron? How many people who are health care professionals in New York do you think are named Leslie Myron? How many people are named Leslie Myron at all?* Was the woman who worked so gently in my mouth for all this time—a woman I so adored—a *murderess?*

I immediately called my mother. She was, of course, beside herself, "Oh my God! Oh my God! You are really some judge of character. I always told you, you pick doctors for the *wrong* reasons. She liked your book, *big deal*. That's why you pick a doctor?

Because she liked your book! This is terrible. This is *really, really,* terrible!"

Me: "Mommy, first of all, innocent until proven guilty. Second of all, she isn't a doctor. She's a hygienist. And third of all, even if she *did* kill her husband, maybe she had a good reason to. And anyway, even if it's true, it's still better than that slovenly hellhole in Queens."

My mother: "Here we go again with Queens! The way you talk about Queens! You don't talk about the private school you went to, the vacations to Europe, all our trips to Israel, skiing in the Alps. I do not like the way you talk about Queens! You give people the wrong idea. You'd think you grew up in the projects."

Me: "Mommy, I *did* grow up in the projects."

At this, my mother went completely wild, screaming: "You did not grow up in the projects!!"

Me: "Okay, fine. I grew up *across the street* from the projects. Either way, I just wanted to let you know what was going on. You say I never call you, so now I'm calling you. And now I'm hanging up because I have to get to the bottom of this. Love you, bye." And then I hung up.

I felt bad getting off the phone so abruptly. I knew my mother hated when I did this, but I also knew she would keep me on the phone for an hour if given the opportunity and I had a crime to solve.

I started to think. I tried to place myself in the mind of the killer, the way the criminologists do, the way Sigourney Weaver had in *Copycat.* I tried to imagine what it feels like to stab someone, let alone what it feels like to stab someone twenty-seven times. That's a lot of times to stab someone. Shit, *one* time is a lot of times to stab someone.

I imagined Leslie, with her sparkling, bright-white teeth attacking Mervin.

I imagined her saying things like, "Mervin, you motherfucker!"

I imagined her covered in fresh blood.

Then, washing the blood off herself.

Then I imagined her, after the fact, looking in the mirror, opening her mouth and examining her teeth and methodically flossing one tooth after the other. I wondered what provoked her. Had Mervin been abusive? Was Leslie a sociopath like successful San Francisco businessman Scott Peterson, who hacked up his pregnant wife without a shred of remorse? You know, they're always the ones you least expect. This was pretty gnarly stuff, even for the most seasoned investigators. I wondered if I should call the police. After about an hour of surfing the Internet and another hour of perusing the FBI's website to see if there were any job openings, my phone rang. It was my mother, *again*.

Me: "Yes, Mommy?"

My mother: "I just wanted to let you know how upset I am by this whole thing."

Me: "Oh, don't worry, everything is fine. I found her."

My mother: "What do you mean, you found her?"

Me: "I mean exactly what I said. What part of 'I found her' confused you? She got another job, she's working for Dr. Bogdanovich, and she thinks he's a very nice man."

My mother: "Very good, Peri. I'm glad you think this is a joke. I don't think this is a joke."

Me: "I don't think it's a joke either. You should be thrilled. You said my teeth needed to be cleaned and now they're going to get cleaned. I'm seeing her next week."

Since my mother didn't know I had just gotten my teeth cleaned by Marabelle, I could really keep this going.

My mother: "You're doing *what!*"

Me: "I'm seeing her next week."

My mother: "What! You are *not.*"

Me: "I am."

My mother: "You. Are. *Not.* Going. *Please.*"

Me: "I am."

My mother, who may or may not have started to realize how ridiculous this was: "Peri, please. I don't believe you. I don't believe someone hired her."

I wasn't letting it go so easily. I was enjoying myself too much.

Me: "No one hired her. She's working out of her apartment."

My mother: "You're out of your mind. You can't be so crazy. I'm telling you right now that you're *not* going to see Leslie. You're not going to her apartment with all those sharp instruments. God only knows what she is liable to do."

Me: "Don't worry, Mommy, it's not an apartment. It's an attached house."

My mother, screaming: "This is not safe! This is *not* safe!"

I hadn't laughed so hard in a very long time.

The truth, of course, was that I hadn't located Leslie. I had no idea where she was and, to this day, as far as I know she is still at large. I tried pressing Dr. Mulligatani at a follow-up visit and the only thing he would say was that she was "nut goot for de office." In the end, it would be Veronica who spilled the beans. Leslie *had* allegedly killed her husband, but that wasn't why she was fired. She was fired because she had stolen more than a quarter of a million dollars from the business *and* was a raging cokehead. Veronica told me she started to get suspicious about the coke when Leslie would spontaneously get nosebleeds. And then, in the coup de grace, Veronica found her hovered over the nitrous machine blowing lines!

My mother, who has never so much as smoked a joint in her life: "Oh, you really have some sense of judgment!"

Me: "You kind of really have to admire her chutzpah."

My mother: "There is really something wrong with you."

My mother can say what she wants. There isn't a goddamn thing wrong with me. If I'm not mistaken, *I'm* the one who is constantly pointing out that people are rarely what they seem. If you look at the facts, what do *I* really do? I sit around and write. It's everyone else who's out there doing fucked-up shit.

I was like, "Mommy, you're the one who's always telling me that I should pick a doctor because they are good at what they do. What do I care if Leslie stole money? If she does a little coke here and there? She's the best dental hygienist I've ever had. Jesus, it's not like she killed someone!"

My mother was silent.

I go, "Okay, so maybe you're right. Maybe she *did* kill someone. But no one ever proved that and even if she *did* kill someone, it doesn't take away from the fact that she is a great hygienist. You can't be so closed minded."

Again, Noam's sage advice came to mind: People are complicated. They're multifaceted. They can be more than one thing. Things aren't black-and-white. Plus, Leslie was a Jew! Innocent until proven guilty!

5

CASUAL ENCOUNTERS

My mother was probably right to be worried about me. I had been living at my grandmother's for going on several months and had no resolution in sight. My days were bleak, I didn't really give a shit about anything, and I was subsisting on frozen pizza and espresso. I had spoken to Noam once and I cried the entire time. My main activity was moving from the giant fake king-size bed with the depression in the middle of it to the plastic-covered pink couch and back again. And with the exception of when I absolutely had to go out for work, I did nothing but watch television.

Hanna, seeing what a sorry state I was in, convinced me that what I needed was a night out. She had friends in town and persuaded me to go with her to meet them at a bar. I should have known better than to take advice from Hanna, but it was just more evidence of how poor my decision-making skills had become. None of the guys were particularly good-looking but one of them, Steve, honed in on me from the second I arrived and began hitting on me. I wasn't at all attracted to him but I was feeling particularly self-loathing so I went with it. Plus, he was Jewish, so I figured he was harmless. I've always been wary of strange men but I'm less wary of strange men who are Jewish since, statistically, Jewish men are rarely serial killers. Plus, Steve had just moved to New York from Canada and Canadians, by nature, are generally fairly innocuous.

After a few drinks, I started to let my guard down. I was getting drunker and he was getting cuter, which is generally how these things work. I ordered another drink. We made out for a few minutes at the bar and I decided I may as well take him home with me. I think it's fair to say that anyone who is making out with some guy she just met in a bar when she isn't even really attracted to him is probably not in an especially good place in her life. I think it's also fair to say that someone who then proceeds to take that guy back to her apartment, especially the home of a recently deceased relative is *definitely*, *definitely* not in a good place.

The incredible thing was that I was such a disaster that this didn't even *occur* to me. Like, oh, I don't know, maybe it's kind of weird to bring some random guy back to your dead grandmother's house when it's filled with all your dead grandmother's shit and that maybe, just *maybe* it's kind of creepy to fuck someone in your dead grandmother's bed. The thought didn't even cross my mind. I told Hanna I would call her in the morning and, with Steve in tow, hailed a taxi.

During the ride, Steve started to tell me about how he had just gotten out of a very long relationship and how he had finally broken it off because his girlfriend wasn't Jewish.

I was like, "No offense, but you are seriously ruining the moment here. I just picked you up in a bar. Do you really think I want to hear about your failed personal relationships?"

By the time we got back to the apartment complex, I was more than a little wary. To boot, when I tried to open the front door of the apartment, my key didn't work. I was sure I had been locked out. Every month I would send a rent check in and pray I would not come home to an eviction notice on the door. So far, so good. But now, of all times, I couldn't get my key in the door. *Those Tishman Speyer motherfuckers*, I thought. *They changed the locks*. I started to panic. Steve was so dumb he didn't even notice. It took about five whole minutes before I realized that I was on the wrong floor. My life was becoming more and more pathetic by the minute.

Oh, if my grandmother could see me now. She'd be rolling over in her grave, I thought as I lit a cigarette in her living room. I sat down on the couch and Steve sat across from me, on the piano bench. In case I forgot to mention this earlier, the piano was another one of the "antiques" we were trying to sell. Uncle Bark was convinced it was worth thousands of dollars. I was fairly certain we weren't going to be able to give it away. Steve was like, "Wow, this place is really interesting. Do you live here alone?"

Me: "It's one of the properties I inherited from my great-aunt and I'm staying here while we auction off her stuff."

Steve ran his hand along the piano and said, "Oh, wow. That's really cool. So all this stuff is, like, antique?"

Me: "Yeah, totally. The piano you're sitting at is really rare. Christie's has a Russian oligarch who is really interested."

Steve: "It's really cool. My ex-girlfriend used to play the piano."

After some more strained small talk and me spewing even more nonsense, Steve started droning on again about his ex-girlfriend and the Jewish thing until I was finally like, "Can you please shut the fuck up? It's like four in the morning and I'm really not in the mood to play Dr. Freud."

He eventually made his way over to me and we started hooking up on the plastic-covered pink couch I had been languishing on for so many months. I realized that the couch had probably never seen so much action in its entire life. I also realized that Steve was kind of fat, which I hadn't noticed earlier.

Why, oh why, hadn't I just stayed home and watched *Law and Order*? I could always count on Ice-T for a good night. I had become increasingly fond of his character, Fin Tutuola. As Steve maneuvered his hand up my shirt, I began thinking about a recent episode when he said to a criminal he had arrested, "You have the right to an attorney and if you throw up in my car, I'll kill ya." That really cracked me up. I was also obsessed with his real-life wife, Coco, who had made a cameo appearance in that episode. In real life, Coco was famous for, among other things, her prominent camel toe.

Steve, of course, had no way of knowing that I was fantasizing about Coco's camel toe and took my pause as an opportunity to take his shirt off. I was horrified, absolutely horrified, to see that he was covered—absolutely covered—with hair. When I say hair, I don't mean regular dude body hair like most guys have. Steve was covered in coarse, pubic-like hair. And he looked like a fat horse. If that weren't bad enough, he also smelled like a barnyard animal. It was eminently clear to me that under absolutely no circumstances was I going to have sex with this guy.

Steve, of course, had other ideas.

But when he realized there was no chance I was going to fuck him, he changed direction. In one of the most shameless displays I have *ever* borne witness to, with absolutely no warning whatsoever, Steve removed his maple-leaf-covered boxer shorts, exposed more of his fat, hairy body along with his revolting short, stubby dick, and began to masturbate.

As if my life weren't pathetic enough, I now had a plump, hirsute Canadian man stroking his penis on my grandmother's couch.

Let me make something clear. An invitation to come back to someone's apartment (or their dead grandmother's apartment, as the case may be) is not a promise of anything. And it certainly doesn't give you carte blanche to jerk off. I will grant you that if someone takes you home at four in the morning it's safe to assume that there will probably be some sexual activity going on, but you really never know.

Despite my displeasure, Steve continued to jerk himself off and actually sat there masturbating until he ejaculated, like a zoo gorilla, all over himself and simultaneously all over the couch. I silently thanked God for the plastic cover, jumped out of the way just in time to avoid getting hit and ran into the bathroom.

I inspected myself to make sure his vile emission was nowhere on me and though it seemed I had made it in the nick of time, I took a quick shower just to be sure. By the time I returned to the living room, Steve had somehow made it from the couch to the floor where he was passed out and *snoring*. My life had reached an all-time low.

My AA friends tell me that you have to hit rock bottom before you can ascend again. I was fairly certain that having an overweight, hairy Canadian stranger curled up naked and snoring on my dead grandmother's Persian-style area rug was definitely my rock bottom.

I began kicking him in his fat, hairy side. When he finally woke up I told him it was time to go.

Apparently *I'd* offended *him*. "Are you always this nasty?" Steve asked as he walked out of the apartment. I yelled after him, "If things don't work out with the Russian oligarch, I'll let you know about the piano. Maybe you can buy it for your ex-girlfriend!"

I called Hanna at like nine the next morning. "Come over. Now. Please."

When she got there, I was like, "Your friend Steve is the most disgusting person I have ever hooked up with in my entire life." By the time I got to the end of the story, she was doubled over laughing. "I want you to know that I hold you responsible for this. You know I shouldn't be around people right now."

Hanna, still laughing: "I'm sorry, I'm sorry! You're right. I'll make it up to you."

Me: "I can't imagine how you're going to make this up to me."

Hanna: "I can make it up to you right now. I have a few stories I think might cheer you up."

Me: "This better be good."

Hanna: "It is."

Me: "Well, get to it."

Hanna: "Okay. Okay. I met someone."

Me: "Oh my God! You did? Last night?"

Hanna: "No, no! When I got home last night. I was bored and I went on Craigslist . . ."

Me: "This is already a great story. I love it when you meet people on Craigslist. Go on."

Hanna: "I met an Indian guy who wants to shave me."

Me: "Excuse me?"

Hanna: "I'm serious."

Me: "What do you mean, *he wants to shave you*? He wants to shave your legs? He wants to shave your pussy?"

I do not believe I would let a stranger near my genital area with a razor blade. But then, too, I do not believe I would allow a masseur to stick his fingers in my anus, but either way.

Hanna: "He wants to shave my tits."

Me: "Oh. My. God. You just made my fucking day."

Hanna: "Hmm. I did? You really *should* get out more."

Me: "*I* should get out more? You're trolling Craigslist and talking to some Indian guy who wants to shave your tits and you're telling *me I* should get out more? Who ever even heard of such a thing?"

Hanna: "Maybe Indian women have hairy tits?"

Me: "That's the stupidest thing I've ever heard in my life."

Hanna: "And then, there was another guy I talked to who wants me to nurse him."

Me: "What do you mean, he wants you to *nurse* him?"

Hanna: "He told me that he's been fantasizing about suckling from a woman's breast for years and he doesn't care if there is milk or no milk but if there *isn't* milk, he is willing to work at suckling to see if by doing so, I will start to produce milk."

Me: "*Please* tell me you're kidding."

Hanna: "I'm not! He even said we could get a breast pump! I don't know how these people find me!"

I was beginning to think that maybe Hanna actually might have the same brain disorder that Dr. Zarkin, who carved his initials into his patients, had. I mean what would it take to realize that *she* was the common denominator here.

Me: "So are you going to have sex with one of these people?"

Hanna: "I don't think so."

Me: "Why not?"

Hanna: "I don't know any of them. It would be too weird."

Me: "You didn't know your masseur either."

Hanna: "That wasn't having sex."

Me: "Well, neither is letting someone shave your tits!"

Hanna: "I know. But still, I don't think I want to do that. And anyway, this hot guy, who I met last year, e-mailed me."

Me: "Yeah? How did you meet this one?"

Hanna: "Match.com."

Me: "Why did I even bother asking? And . . ."

Hanna: "And we had e-mail sex."

Me: "You had *e-mail* sex? What the fuck is e-mail sex?"

Hanna: "It's like phone sex, but over e-mail. I thought we were going to hang out in person, but after e-mail sex, he was done. I told him I wanted to *see* him, and he promised that we would meet, but then he couldn't even commit to that!"

Me: "How did this all begin, please?"

Hanna: "He e-mailed me but hinted that he didn't want to or have time to date. So basically, he was e-mailing me because he wanted to get laid."

Me: "So that would have been perfect, if all you want to do is get laid."

Hanna: "I know but it kind of pissed me off that he said that. I was going to send him the perfect 'fuck you' e-mail and then I changed my mind. And so, for a few nights, we had e-mail sex. I was sending him pictures of myself, he was sending me pictures of himself, we were talking about what we would do to each other, and then when I told him I wanted to see him, he disappeared. I guess he was satisfied with that. I must give good e-mail sex."

Me: "Hanna, I know I'm not really in a position to judge and don't get mad, but I feel it incumbent upon me to say this: maybe you should consider the fact that if what you want is to have an *actual* relationship, or even *actual* sex, maybe, *just maybe* you shouldn't be having *virtual* sex with a *virtual* stranger."

Hanna, missing the point as usual: "He wasn't a stranger. I met him last year."

Me: "Whatever. Fine, You know what I'm saying. Fine, he wasn't a perfect stranger. I'm not trying to argue semantics with you."

This girl never ceases to amaze me. It's like it's one thing if what you want to do is have e-mail sex, which, to begin with, sounds like the biggest waste of time in the world, but fine. If all you want to do is have e-mail sex, then God bless you. But Hanna didn't want to have e-mail sex. Hanna wanted to have *actual* sex. And then she goes and does something like this and then she's disappointed that she's not having actual sex. Or she's having casual sex with someone and then she's disappointed that whoever she is having casual sex with doesn't want to be her boyfriend. It's like you can't do one thing when what you really want to do is something else. If you want to have e-mail sex, then have e-mail sex. But have e-mail sex because that, in and of itself, is what you want. If you want to get laid, then for the love of God, go out and get laid. If you want a boyfriend, I don't know what to tell you.

Actually, I take that back. If you want a boyfriend, stop wanting a boyfriend. Life doesn't work like that. If you want a boyfriend, start with forming a good relationship with yourself instead of looking to other people to fulfill you. Stop accepting things you don't want. Stop settling. If you don't wait for what you want, you're never going to get it. That may sound like some sort of new age garbage but it isn't and I know it isn't because I'm not into new age garbage. These are just facts. Have some fucking self-respect. Have a little faith in yourself. Have a little self-esteem.

And for the love of God, know that you're not going to find a boyfriend in the Casual Encounters section of fucking Craigslist. Or shit, I don't know. Maybe you are, but it seems unlikely at best. I don't know what to tell you. That's been my experience at least. You find things in the most unexpected places. Specifically, when you're not looking for them. And sometimes, dare I say *most of the time*, things don't work out how you think they will.

If only I could have taken this advice myself, I would have been golden. But hindsight is always twenty-twenty. At the time, I was blind as a fucking bat.

6

OFF THE DEEP END

As though my debacle with Steve weren't bad enough, it was child's play compared to what happened next. I took self-destructive to a whole new level. There is a reason they say that the quickest way to end a friendship is with sex—because it is.

Nico was, well, everything. He was my best friend, my closest confidant, and technically he was even sort of my boss. We had been attracted to each other from the moment we met, but I was still with Noam and nothing had happened. But from the moment we started to work together we pretty much became inseparable.

Nico, among other mogulesque things, owned a major ad agency. He had offices in New York, London, Paris, and Tokyo. He was born in South Africa and grew up between Johannesburg and London and was now based in New York and Paris. He had convinced me to do some freelance consulting, which was kind of a dream come true. I was writing copy and designing for major ad campaigns without any of the commitment that usually accompanies working for a major corporation. And because it was Nico's company, he could do whatever he wanted. And what he wanted was me.

This went on for three years until Noam and I broke up—at which point Nico almost immediately made his move. Maybe, if the timing and circumstances had been different, we would have stood a chance and things would have worked out, but that's not what happened. We were kind of doomed from the get-go. Nico adored me as much as I adored him, but he just wanted to have a good time. I, being in a deep, dark depression, was looking for someone to save me. And I was hoping it would be him. This, of course, was a recipe for disaster. And the harder I tried, the more of a mess it became.

I'd be just as happy, if not happier, if I could forget that any of this ever happened, because quite frankly it was fucking mortifying. In short order, I was crazy, I was depressed, and I was obsessed. For all intents and purposes, I was also sleeping with my boss. Nico, for his part, was trying to temper my insanity by distancing himself from me whenever he could but it wasn't working. In fact, it was entirely possible that he was making it worse. He made it abundantly clear from the beginning that he was not interested in getting into a relationship, but he was also sending me mixed messages.

I nevertheless adored him. He was smart and funny and successful and stylish and he knew what I was about to say before I said it and we cracked each other up. And we drank together and we partied together and we just had fun together. He knew everyone and he traveled all the time and each day was a new adventure. And while sometimes that's awesome, sometimes it's not.

When everything else in your life is up in the air, taking one of your most stable relationships and turning it into a hot mess is not the best move. And I may have been a disaster, but Nico wasn't helping. One minute he was all over me and the next minute he was telling me he didn't want to be accountable to me. Any normal person would have headed for the hills, but I had some deluded notion that he would eventually come around and his actions weren't helping, so I just couldn't let it go.

We'd be out, having a great time, and we couldn't keep our hands off each other. And I would always think that tonight—whatever night tonight was—would be the night that he would tell me how in love he was with me. But it was the same story every time. At the very last second, Nico would make up some nonsensical excuse about how he had to go home or be up really early or he had a meeting or he was really tired or he had a hangnail. One night I actually pulled him aside and was like, "Listen, I know that you're in love with me and you're just scared."

And he was straight up like, "Uh, not really, P. To be honest, I'm not really sure what I want."

You would think that with all the advice I had been doling out to Hanna that I would have been less of a fool. You'd be wrong.

The debacle started a few months after Noam and I broke up. Nico and I went to a big industry event together. There was a photo booth there. And in the pictures of us we're sticking our tongues out; we're laughing. In one of the photos, he is biting my nose. The sexual energy is almost tangible. This was typical behavior.

After the event, we went back to my apartment and were lying on Grandma's couch playing around when suddenly something switched. He looked at me and touched my face in a way that he never had before and seconds later we were kissing. In that moment, I remember feeling something I hadn't felt in months—hope. It was the first time since Noam and I had broken up that I felt something other than utter despair. In that moment, Nico became my life raft. I would have fucked him right then and there but he slowed me down—which, incidentally, was also fairly mortifying.

Nico, like Noam, was a good deal older than I was. And he had the foresight to know that I was in a very dark place. He also knew that unless two people have a conversation to ensure that they are on exactly the same page, hooking up with your best friend is usually not a good idea under the *best* of circumstances. He also knew that hooking up with your best friend who you work with and who just broke up with her boyfriend of ten years is just plain stupid.

For my part, I had replaced all of the misery that goes along with a breakup with total mania. I was elated. In other words, I pretty much went off the deep end. It was much easier to be obsessed with this new "relationship" than it was to mourn the loss of my last one. The problem, of course, was that there *was* no new relationship. Nico had made it very clear that the last thing he wanted to do was to be my boyfriend. But I wasn't interested in pesky things like facts. I was certain that he was the solution to all my problems. And so each time he would call me and tell me he was in town, I would jump like a small lapdog, convinced that sooner or later he would see the light.

It was pathetic.

I was pathetic.

I began writing him the kinds of letters psychologists recommend you write but never send. The only difference was I was actually *sending* them.

Nico,

There is no other way to say this . . . I'm leaving.
It's an incredibly difficult decision, but I think it's the right
one. Or maybe it's not the right one, but it's the only one.
Most simply, around you is not a healthy place for me to be.
I don't want to, but I'm leaving. A few months ago, when
you said you don't know what you want, I told you I didn't
believe you. I said, I think you do know what you want,
that I believe you know exactly what you want, but that
you're scared. Now, I'm not sure I was right. I think I may
have overestimated how well I know you, or, more likely,
I was blinded by belief—in you, in me, in us. I see now,
that you were telling me the truth—you really don't know
what you want. Or, you do, but it's not me, it's not us, it's
not the vision I've had in my head. I think I've filled a very
important void for you. And you filled one for me, too. But
I don't want to keep filling your void because it makes mine
bigger. So there really is nothing else to do—but leave. I'm
sorry to, because I've so very deeply enjoyed our time together.
And I wish you nothing but happiness, but not at the expense
of my own. It makes me so sad because I deeply believe that
we could have been so great together or, rather, that we are so
great together, but the truth is, that we're not together. And
it seems clear to me, very clear, that we're not going to be.
So I wish you the best of luck. And I hope we can, one day,
reconnect.

It was like the theater of the ridiculous, because less than
a week after sending these nonsensical letters, it would be as
though nothing happened and I'd be right where I started.

During the height of all of this drama, Nico was going to

have knee surgery. He had just sold his apartment in New York and was in the process of buying a loft in Tribeca, so he was living in a hotel on the Upper East Side. Two nights before his surgery, we were having dinner there and we had a big fight. I was adamant that I wanted to take him to the hospital and stay with him during his surgery so I could nurse him back to health. And he was adamant about *not* wanting me to take him to the hospital and *not* wanting me to stay with him and *not* wanting me to nurse him back to health. And I was irate. So after dinner, in the lobby of his hotel, I said, "I'm leaving." I was hoping he would say, "No, stay." But, of course, he didn't say that. He didn't say anything close to that. In fact, he was probably thrilled to get rid of me.

Instead of leaving, like anyone with even a shred of self-respect would have, I announced, "You know what? Actually, I'm going to stay. I'm spending the night."

And so I spent the night with him. Again. I woke up the next morning thinking everything was just peachy, thinking that because he went down on me all of our issues had dissipated into thin air. And when the subject of the hospital came up again, I just assumed that he had changed his mind. When he articulated, for the ninety-seventh time, that he *still* did not want me to take him to the hospital the next day, I flipped. I was like, "I don't know what the fuck your problem is, but I'm sick of this bullshit."

I marched out of the hotel room and swore to myself all day long that I would never speak to him again. By the time I fell asleep that night I almost had myself convinced.

At six o'clock the next morning, I woke up to my phone ringing. It was Nico.

Nico: "I'm sorry I acted like an asshole. Will you please come meet me at the hospital?"

Me: "I'm sorry, who is this?"

Nico: "Come on, P, really. Please."

Me: "You're breaking up. I can't hear a word you're saying. I think I heard an 'I'm sorry' but I couldn't really make it out . . ."

Ten minutes later, I was in a taxi on my way to the hospital. Then, while he was in surgery, I went to go fill his prescriptions and buy him chicken soup. By the time he woke up, I was sitting at his bedside like a wet nurse, stroking his hand.

There was something about Nico allowing me to see him in such a vulnerable state that just melted my heart. There was also something extremely manipulative about how I inserted myself into this situation. Nico kept saying he didn't want me to be there and I kept pushing him to say yes, knowing that eventually he would cave. Somehow in my twisted logic I figured if I could just get him to say yes more times than he said no, then he'd be my boyfriend and I'd be able to avoid dealing with my life—which, I admit, is *psychotic*.

And if I told you that the man had transformed into an *angel*, it would be a grave understatement. If I told you that I had become more delusional than ever about the nature of our relationship and where it was headed, it would be an even more grave understatement.

After two days of recuperating in the hospital, I went with him back to his hotel. I was like a pig in shit, more certain than ever that Nico had finally seen the light. I stayed with him that whole week, bringing him frozen bags of peas in the middle of the night to ice his knee and replacing them when they were no longer cold enough. I even tied his shoes so he didn't have to bend down. And then, one morning as I was on my way out, he said, "I love you."

Nico and I had said "I love you" to each other hundreds if not thousands of times, but neither one of us had dared to say it since we started "seeing" each other, for lack of a better term. Neither one of us ever mentioned it and even though nothing had changed, I felt like this incident had *deep meaning*. In my own defense, I wasn't entirely wrong. It *did* have deep meaning—in my head.

In perhaps what was my first real moment of clarity, I decided I needed to take control of my life and that maybe what I needed was just some good old-fashioned therapy. This was a huge step for me. I had always thought therapy was kind of a joke. I had never seen a therapist before and have always operated under the impression that not only do I not *need* therapy but also that going to therapy was a self-indulgent, whiny, New York Jew thing to do. I mean even in the worst of times (and these were certainly them), what was so bad in my life? People were dying of AIDS and malaria and cholera and extreme drug-resistant tuberculosis. You think *they* went to therapy? Therapy was a luxury for people who didn't *really* have problems. Nevertheless, I had to admit that while relatively speaking I didn't *really* have problems, I definitely had problems.

Plus, I wasn't convinced it would be that helpful. All I had to do was look at Hanna and see how much good it had done her. She had, like, three therapy appointments a week and she was even more dysfunctional than I was. But I really was at the end of my rope. So instead of calling one of the hundreds of people I knew to recommend someone, I did what was arguably the stupidest thing in the world. I went online.

To begin with, finding anything in a frantic late-night search on the Internet is never a good idea, let alone a therapist and let alone when you're as paranoid as I am. But there I was at two in the morning digging around the depths of the World Wide Web for some assistance. I had decided that if I were going to see a therapist, I definitely needed a gay. I've been around the block enough times to know that there is only one thing straight men think about when they have a vulnerable, attractive woman in their clutches—blow jobs. Beyond that, straight men aren't exactly renowned for their listening skills.

And that brought up another problem. I'll give you a tip here and potentially save you some time. If you look up "gay therapist" on the Internet, you're not going to find a gay therapist. What you are going to find is a therapist who specializes in helping *gay people*. It's like trying to find a gay dentist. Health care professionals do not share the intimate details of their personal lives. It's not like, "Hi, I'm Dr. So-and-So. I specialize in anxiety disorders, and at night, I like to be blindfolded, bent over, and fucked up the ass."

Indeed, the only people who disclose their sexual orientation and preferences are people who are selling sexual services. So, while I did finally find a therapist, I could tell immediately by his photo that he was not a homosexual. It was obvious, for starters, by the poor lighting and tacky clothes. Also, a gay would have never used such an unflattering photo of himself. This was disappointing, but it was the best I could come up with. Plus, there was some stuff on his website that jumped out at me: "You deserve to be happy. We all go through times in our lives where we are down and we need to share our feelings with others. Let us help."

And: "You can have your life full again. You are not broken. You are not damaged for life. You are in a place where it is hard to see a way out. We can help. We can help you build the life you really deserve." Suddenly, I understood how Hanna had fallen for her masseur.

As I was walked over to his office, I thought, *I do deserve to be happy! I do want my life back!* But then, I started wondering, *Who even knows if this guy is a real doctor?* I mean I could place an ad on the Internet claiming I were a therapist or a doctor and really, without some serious investigating, who would be the wiser? There was a real chance he had placed that ad in hopes of luring a victim to his lair.

In a moment of genius, I decided to leave evidence on the sidewalk in front of the entrance to his building. I reasoned that the smartest thing would be a piece of identification, but I wasn't about to toss my driver's license. I lit a cigarette and tried to think. *Duh.* I finished my cigarette and left the butt right under the buzzers. Now, if I disappeared, at least the police would have something with my DNA on it. This would help them create a timeline of my last-known whereabouts, which they would need to piece together the events that led up to my disappearance. Watching so much *Law & Order* was clearly paying off.

I loved the idea that I was an active participant in helping the police find me. I wanted them to know that I left the butt there specifically for them, so I picked it up, took a pen out of my bag and wrote "PA" on it. Then I texted Hanna the address and told her where I was going. If something terrible *did* happen, I hoped she would be able to pull her pussy off the Internet for long enough to make herself useful.

The moment I walked into the office, I knew things were not going to work out. There was dust everywhere and the furniture was cheap and worn. How was I supposed to heal when my aesthetic sensibilities were being offended at every turn?

I realized that my first instinct was, in fact, correct. I did need a gay. If I were going to disclose personal information about myself to a complete stranger, I wanted to feel some sort of connection. I needed to be able to feel like I could relate on some level. With a gay, at least I knew we were coming from the same universe. At the very least, I knew that culturally we'd have something in common—like an eye for aesthetics or a scathing sense of humor or perhaps even a penchant for designer clothing.

Clearly M. F. Benning and I were not off to a great start. I was having a hard time getting over the fact that his first name wasn't really even a name. I was always skeptical of people who didn't have real names. What name in the world could be worse than using M. F. as your name? I was tempted to ask if people ever called him Motherfucker, but I restrained myself.

Even though I was trying to keep an open mind, it was clear to me that we were doomed. But I was determined to persevere. I told M. F. that my entire life, as I knew it, had come apart before my very eyes. That even though I was the one responsible for tearing it apart, I was still suffering terribly.

M. F. fingered his goatee, looked at me dead in the eyes, and I swear to God, said, "Are you an alcoholic?"

I really think my eyes nearly popped out of my head. I said, "I'm sorry? Did you just ask me if I was an alcoholic?"

M. F. Benning, as though this were the most linear jump in the world, said, "Yes, I did. *Are* you an alcoholic?"

I don't have any academic qualification in psychology or psychiatry or psychotherapy, but I'm fairly fucking certain that nothing I said or did suggested in any way, shape, or form or gave any indication or impression *whatsoever* that I was suffering from alcoholism. Depression, maybe, but alcoholism? I was like, "I just told you that I've been sitting on the couch for nine months eating frozen pizza and watching *Law and Order*. I did not just tell you that I have been sitting on the couch for nine months drinking scotch until I blacked out. Do I *look* like I'm an alcoholic? Do I have blown-out blood vessels crawling all over the tip of my nose? Do I *smell* like I'm an alcoholic? Given that I'm pouring my soul out to you, baring the most humiliating details about my life, don't you think that if I were here because I were an alcoholic, I'd be *telling* you that I'm an alcoholic?"

M. F. Benning didn't say anything.

"Look, I'm not trying to play games with you over here. I *know* what's wrong with me. I've just told you, in a very articulate way, exactly what's wrong with me. I'm not trying to figure out what my problems are. I *know* what my problems are. I'm trying to figure out how to make them better and given the fact that I'm a fairly intelligent human being, I thought it might be prudent to seek the assistance of a professional."

M. F. Benning continued to sit there, staring at me like a cat.

What do you do with a person like that? You can't do *anything* with a person like that. I wanted to scream, "I'm talking to you. Don't just sit there and nod your head. *Do* something. *Say* something insightful. Give me some sage advice. For the love of God, aren't you a therapist? Isn't that the point? Aren't you supposed to *give* me therapy? This is not supposed to be a passive exercise. I'm not here to listen to myself speak. I do that all day long. I'm a writer, for God's sake. It's not like I don't know what's going on; it's not like I'm not introspective. I know exactly what is going on and what's going on is that I'm fucked-up and I'm becoming *more* fucked-up, which is why I schlepped all the way over here and if you could do something to help me, it would be greatly appreciated. If not, please let me know so I can find someone who can. Thanks so much."

Even though I was feeling homicidal, I tried to articulate this in a less aggressive fashion. I was like, "Listen, I know my life isn't that bad. I know that all things considered my life is pretty great. I'm not dying; I wasn't molested as a child; I haven't been raped; I'm not homeless; I'm not starving; the list goes on. I know I have a lot to be thankful for. I know that what Anaïs Nin said is true: 'We see the world as we are, not as it is.' I am aware of all of this. And yet I am *still* suffering."

And then I threw some of the stuff that was on his website in for good measure. I said, "Like it says on your website, I think I'm just in a place where it is hard to see a way out and I just need some help."

M. F. Benning opened and closed his eyes and said, "I think I can help you."

I looked at him expectantly.

He said, "Have you ever had green tea?"

Not following, I was like, "Uh, yeah."

M. F. Benning said, "Oh good. Let's make an appointment for next week then."

Needless to say, I walked out of his office more depressed than I was when I arrived. The outlook was fucking bleak.

Part II

7

LIFE IS LIKE A BOWL OF CHERRIES

The one thing—dare I say it felt like the only thing—I had to look forward to was the recent news that my cousin Roy was coming to visit from Tel Aviv. I hadn't seen him in ages and the second I got the news, I pried apart the giant bed so he would have a place to sleep. His timing was perfect, which was not utterly surprising; our histories were intertwined and our lives, in many ways, ran parallel since we were infants. Plus, he had just broken up with his girlfriend, so I knew he'd be the perfect shoulder to cry on.

Because I was an only child, Roy was the closest thing I had ever had to a brother. Our mothers were not biological sisters, but they had grown up in the same one-bedroom apartment in Israel. Our respective grandparents had escaped the Holocaust around the same time and arrived in Israel with very little money and, as such, moved in together.

My grandparents had moved to New York when my mother was thirteen. Roy's mother, Talma, stayed in Israel but she and my mother kept in touch. Roy and I were born the same year, one month apart. My parents took me to Israel for the first time when I was three years old and from then on, we went back every summer and we always stayed with Roy and his parents, Talma and Yochanan. They were as much my family as my own. They had a beautiful house in the suburbs outside Tel Aviv with the most amazing backyard and garden I had ever seen. Growing up, it was my home away from home. Because of this connection to a faraway land, I always felt like I had something special, something that other people didn't have. I'm not sure what it was—maybe roots, or history, or a unique connection to a foreign place, maybe all of the above. Israel was the polar opposite of New York but I always felt at home there and unlike in New York, I was free to roam about. Even as a kid, I could walk alone outside without having to worry that I would be kidnapped and I could walk barefoot without having to worry that I would step on an AIDS-infected needle. Wild flowers grew everywhere and the scent of honeysuckle was so strong that it made me dizzy. The sun was always shining, you could go to the beach almost year-round, and the food was the freshest I had ever tasted.

I thought Israel was a magical place and when I was there, I didn't have a care in the world. And as long as there were no bombs going off it *was* a magical place, but as a little girl I didn't know about things like suicide bombers and precarious political situations. I only knew that there was the sea and the earth and the flowers and I had Talma and Yochanan's backyard and I had Roy, my partner in crime.

Also, my mother had insisted that I attend a Hebrew day school and since I was born, she only spoke to me in Hebrew, so by the time I was about six years old, I was pretty fluent and could converse freely, which only strengthened my bond with Roy and his parents.

Because we were the same age and we were inseparable, everyone thought we were twins. We took all our family vacations together and we went everywhere from Disney World to the Austrian Alps. When we were old enough, our parents foolishly put Roy and me in our own hotel room and we would stay up for hours, drinking, smoking cigarettes, and just generally getting in all sorts of trouble. Once we made a "spa" and flooded a hotel room. But the biggest mess we made was in Munich, when we were sixteen and our parents left us alone on New Year's Eve. To celebrate, we lit firecrackers. Problem was, we were inside and nearly burned down the building. All this is to say that even though we lived on opposite ends of the earth, almost all of my most vivid childhood memories involve Roy and his parents.

When we were eighteen and left home for college, I moved to Arizona and Roy moved to New York, where he became like my parents' surrogate child. By the time I had moved into my grandmother's, it had been several years since we'd seen each other—the longest we had ever gone.

The second Roy walked into my grandmother's apartment, he took a quick look around and was like, "What the fuck is going on here? I can't believe you are living like this. What's wrong with you?"

I filled him in on what a nightmare my life had become and I spared no details. We sat up for hours and drank whiskey and talked and talked and talked. I figured that given the fact that he had just gone through his own breakup, he would be particularly understanding. But Roy is Israeli, which means, among other things, he pulls no punches. He gave it to me straight and he didn't sugarcoat it. He said, "For starters, it's a good thing you broke up with Noam. He was a nice guy, but it was obvious that it was never going to work out. And this bullshit with Nico has got to end. Now."

This may sound harsh and maybe it was, but it was also extremely helpful. I needed a good kick in the ass. And just being around Roy made me feel better. His sheer presence reminded me who I was, where I came from, and I started to have faith that I could become whole again.

The night before he went back to Israel, we went out and got shitfaced. On our way home, at like three in the morning, we were starving, so we stopped at Papaya Dog. I've lived in New York on and off my whole life and had never even stepped foot inside Papaya Dog. It has a very nice healthy-sounding name, which is incredibly misleading because Papaya Dog may well be the most disgusting place on earth. They serve cheap hotdogs that are long and skinny and probably made out of cow anus. But we were trashed and starving and happy to be reunited. We swore that night, over grape soda, that we would never go so long again without seeing each other. By the time Roy went back to Israel, I was in much better shape. In many ways, his visit saved me.

And it was a good thing that I was getting my shit together because I had a huge event coming up and I needed to be on top of my game. This was one of the perks of my job—I got to go to really interesting events and meet really interesting people all the time. Some people were more interesting than others of course, and I'd learned that meeting the people you admire is often a bummer. They are generally shorter, fatter, and uglier than you imagined, but that's neither here nor there.

In this particular scenario, I was being introduced to Philip Roth, my mother's favorite writer, whom I had heard her refer to as "*the* literary lion." And while I've never been particularly starstruck, I flipped when I found out Roth was going to be there. Next thing I know, a mutual friend takes me by the hand, drags me over to Roth, and introduces me to him in this fashion: "Philip. Zis is Periel, she is a grrrreat writer."

I could not imagine anything more humiliating in the entire world. I wanted to curl up in a hole and die. Adding insult to injury, a friend of Roth's who was lingering around us, nodded toward Roth and said to me, "So you like him, huh?"

In attempt to salvage whatever miserly bit of self-respect I had left, I said, "Well, I don't know him, so I can't like *him*, but I do like his work."

This was an out-and-out lie. I had never read a single word Philip Roth had written. Roth, for his part, was sitting at a table with a large bowl of cherries in front him. He looked up from his cherries and stared me up and down, his gaze lingering for a moment too long on my chest. I wasn't wearing a bra and I wondered (and secretly hoped) if in the dim lighting of the restaurant he could make out the faint outline of my nipples. Even at his advanced age, he was quite attractive. I could just imagine my mother's reaction if I told her that I had had sex with Philip Roth.

Roth looked me dead in the eyes and said, "So, you're a great writer, huh?"

I returned his stare and said, "I like to think so."

He looked back down at his bowl of cherries, then back up at me.

He said, "Sit down." And he nodded toward the chair across from him.

I have never followed instructions so quickly in my life.

As I sat, I thought, all the torture and bullshit has finally paid off. I could already envision Roth's endorsement of my next book. Maybe he would say something like, "Periel Aschenbrand is the most brilliant young writer I have ever encountered." Or, "Brilliant, screamingly funny, deeply moving—everything you could hope for in a book." Obviously he wouldn't say something so banal, but that wasn't the point. The point was that I was hanging out with Philip Roth, one of the important living literary figures *of our time*. And that was a big fucking deal.

I was trying to make a good impression and sound mildly intelligent, so I started talking about French critical theory. This was definitely a gamble since I don't actually know anything about French critical theory. Had I read *The Dying Animal* before I met Roth, I would have known this was a colossal waste of time. But I hadn't read *The Dying Animal* before I met Roth because I hadn't read *anything* by Roth before I met him.

As it turned out, it didn't really matter *what* I was talking about because Philip Roth spent the vast majority of the time I was with him alternately talking about his great love for cherries and staring at my tits.

While I was droning on about the great French feminist philosopher Monique Wittig, who is both famous and obscure enough that I thought I could get away with it, Philip Roth interrupted me, "I have a question for you."

I was already formulating my answer. *Yes, Mr. Roth, of course, I would be thrilled to have you write the foreword of my next book.*

I look at him expectantly, the way I imagine a dog would look at its owner right before the owner is about to fill its bowl with food. I was anticipating a very serious literary question.

Roth said, "Do you like cherries?"

Trying not to skip a beat, I licked my lips and batted my eyelashes. "Who doesn't like cherries?" I asked as I smiled sweetly.

Roth got a devilish twinkle in his eye, "Would you like to taste one of my cherries?"

He pierced a cherry with his fork. I opened my mouth, and Philip Roth, one of the greatest writers maybe *ever*, popped a cherry into my mouth.

"Mmmmm," I said, as I smiled at him, "Delicious!"

It was actually revolting. The cherries were preserved in some heavy, sugary red liquid. They tasted like cough syrup. But hey, who was I to ruin an old man's good time?

The whole thing was pretty sexy and I kept wondering if he was going to ask me to come home with him or something but he didn't. He did, however, tell me to "keep in touch" and wrote his address down on a little piece of paper for me. I tucked it snuggly into my bosom and then gave him a sweet, soft kiss good-bye. On the lips, no tongue.

The second I stepped foot outside, I called my mother. I was like, "You are never going to believe who I was just with!"

My mother: "I'm scared to know."

Me: "You shouldn't be. You're going to be thrilled. Philip Roth!"

My mother: "I don't believe you."

Me: "I swear."

My mother: "That's unbelievable!"

Me: "It was unbelievable. It was pretty pornographic, too."

My mother: "Peri, please!"

Me: "What? It was!"

My mother: "What does that mean, it was pornographic?"

Me: "It means that I probably could have slept with him if I wanted to."

My mother: "Oh my God. I can't believe this! That's terrible!"

Me: "Why is that terrible? I thought it was wonderful. I'm

actually sort of regretting that I didn't go home with him. Or to a hotel, that probably would have been better."

My mother: "Peri, are you telling me the truth!?"

Me: "Yes! I swear! I literally just walked out of the restaurant. He even gave me his address."

My mother: "You're telling me that Philip Roth just tried to have sex with you?"

Me: "He didn't exactly *try* to have sex with me, but he was very flirtatious and I could have probably had sex with him if I wanted to. That's all I'm saying."

My mother: "Well, I think that's terrible. A man of his stature shouldn't behave like that."

Me: "Behave like what? I just told you he didn't *do* anything."

My mother: "Yes, but you said he was flirtatious and I would expect him to behave in a more dignified fashion. After all, he's a professor!"

Me: "What does that have to do with anything? Aren't all of his books totally pornographic?"

My mother: "Well, yes, but . . ."

Me: "You don't think I made a mistake by not having sex with him?"

My mother: "Oh my God. Peri, please. No, I do not think you made a mistake by not having sex with him."

Me: "He could catapult my literary career."

My mother: "You can catapult your literary career by yourself with your own talent, not by sleeping with Philip Roth! And isn't he in his seventies!"

Me: "Yeah. So what? Picasso was forty-five when he met Françoise Gilot and she was seventeen."

My mother: "Did he catapult her career?"

Me: "Well, everyone knows who she is, so I guess so."

My mother: "He did not catapult her career. He catapulted her notoriety."

Me: "That's a first step, isn't it?"

My mother: "No, Peri! It is not."

Me: "So you're against sleeping your way to the top?"

My mother: "Yes, I am."

Me: "Well, I'm not and I think I may have made a big mistake. I really think I should have had sex with him."

My mother: "Oh, you are talking such nonsense. Why don't you read one of his books instead of wasting your time with this idiocy!"

Me: "Maybe I'll do both."

My mother: "You are not to sleep with Philip Roth! Do you understand me!?"

The next day I bought every single Philip Roth book I could find. After I finished *Portnoy's Complaint*, I cursed myself again for not sleeping with him. I decided to send him a token of my appreciation and I had the perfect idea for a present. I quickly discerned that Traverse City, Michigan, was world renowned insofar as cherries were concerned. I ordered an enormous crate of them to be delivered to his home and was very pleased with myself.

Once I received confirmation that the package had arrived, I began to obsessively check my mailbox for a thank-you note. I imagined Roth would say something to the effect of how sexy and funny I was, how much he enjoyed meeting me, that he would love to read my book. Whatever he would write, I was certain, would be charming and I would, perhaps, even find a lovely antique frame to display it prominently in my home, if I ever got one.

When people came to visit, they would inevitably ask me what it was. I, of course, would act distracted. "What?" I would ask. They would have to repeat the question and in repeating the question, I would know that they were paying full attention. Only then would I answer. I would pause and strain my neck as though I needed to get a better look at what they were talking about. Maybe I would even giggle a little. Casually I would say, "Oh, *that*, I had no idea what you were talking about. That's just a note from, um, Philip Roth."

Of course, this would impress them immensely. "You know Philip Roth?" Very nonchalantly I would say something vague and interest piquing like, "We've spent a little time together," or maybe even, "We have a mutual friend . . ."

Even though this scenario was absurd, I took solace in my fantasy. Since all else had gone to shit, at least I would have this to remind me of how far I had come. And also because I have never followed the rules, per se, I have taken a lot shit from a lot of people throughout the course of my life. My parents have always been extremely supportive—albeit a bit skeptical—of my decisions. But there are many other people—my parents' friends, other members of my family, the list goes on—who have just been waiting for me to land on my face and crack my skull open for not being more obedient.

It's always been the same story: "Peri is doing *what*? Peri is going *where*?"

Or, as Uncle Bark once said, "You are building your future on a pile of sticks."

I don't blame people for this reaction; we have been bred to be sheep but I refuse to kowtow to convention. It's too boring. In my mind, *not* taking risks has always been a bigger risk than taking them. The sense of security that comes from jobs that confine you to a beige cubicle farm is false. I'd always known that but when Lori's brother, Guy, was killed on September 11, I became more convinced than ever.

And so sometimes it's nice to say to all of the people who have tacitly agreed to live their lives in the most banal, mundane, expected way possible: "And by the way, fuck you. I may be illegally squatting in my dead grandmother's apartment in the East Village, but at least I have a letter from Philip Roth on my wall."

After I sent the cherries, I waited a week.

Then another.

And another.

Eventually, it became painfully obvious that I was waiting in vain. I never even got so much as a cherry pit from him. I don't care *who* you are, if someone sends you two hundred of the best cherries in America, the very least you can do is send them a fucking thank-you note.

Who knows? Maybe I deserved what I got; my intentions were not exactly pure to begin with. And you know what Sir Walter Scott says. Or maybe you don't know what Sir Walter Scott says. I'll tell you what Sir Walter Scott says. He says, "Oh what a tangled web we weave / When first we practice to deceive."

And really, who am I to argue?

Right when I thought things were taking a turn for the better, they took a turn for the worse. And then, they got worse yet. After it was eminently clear that I was never going to hear from Philip Roth again, I received an e-mail from Andrew Wylie. Anyone who knows anything about the book world knows that Andrew Wylie is the most powerful and ruthless literary agent in the world. He represents the biggest names in the industry—dead and alive—everyone from Nabokov to Rushdie. I couldn't imagine what he wanted with me.

And then it hit me. Wylie was Philip Roth's agent. Roth was *finally* reaching out.

I opened the e-mail. It read:

Andrew Wylie and Lady Susie Sainsbury
Invite you to dinner in honor of
Michael Boyd
Artistic Director of the Royal Shakespeare Company
On
Thursday, June 19, 2008
Drinks 7:15 PM
Dinner 8:00 PM
Dress Code: Business attire, ties required

And there he was, God, in all his glory, smiling upon me. I had no idea who Lady Susie Sainsbury was, what the Royal Shakespeare Company was, or even who Michael Boyd was, and to be frank, I didn't really give a shit.

I wondered if I could bring a guest? Maybe I would bring Nico? No, that was a terrible idea. It would obviously be better to bring a girlfriend. Maybe Hanna? Certainly two good-looking women are better than one. I wondered if Roth would be at this dinner. Then I chided myself for having floundered in my self-confidence. Obviously Roth himself had suggested I would be a good addition to what was obviously going to be a very exclusive literary event.

I didn't want to RSVP from my personal e-mail address since the e-mail seemed to be from someone at his agency rather than from Wylie personally. I decided to be clever and respond as though I were *my* assistant responding on my own behalf. This would send a clear message that they were dealing with someone who was very important in her own right.

I wrote:

Periel Aschenbrand would be pleased to attend dinner and drinks on June 19. She has asked me to convey to Andrew that she thanks him for the invitation and looks forward to meeting him.

Sincerely,

Julia Mead, Executive Assistant to

Periel Aschenbrand

I hit SEND.

Then I sent *another* e-mail that said, "Please confirm receipt of this e-mail," so it would seem like my assistant was really on top of her shit.

And *then* I started planning my outfit.

I was thinking sexy, but chic, and that perhaps I'd wear my high-waisted black pants, with suspenders and the lace Christian Louboutin spike heels that Nico bought me for my birthday last year. I pulled out a strand of Chanel pearls. I thought, *This necklace will provide just the right touch to balance rock and roll with downtown chic*—which is often how I regard my sense of style.

I tried everything on.

I looked in the mirror.

I thought, *You look perfect*.

I took everything off and hung the outfit on a hanger.

I hadn't felt so good in a very long time.

Ever so pleased with myself, I sauntered back over to my desk and logged back in to my e-mail account.

I saw that I had received an e-mail from the reception desk of Mr. Wylie again. I thought, *How lovely. He probably told his secretary to personally reach out to me immediately and tell me he was looking forward to meeting me as well.*

I clicked OPEN. The e-mail read as follows:

Many thanks for your e-mail.

Unfortunately, Mr. Wylie and Lady Sainsbury's invitation seems to have been misdirected to your account. It was not intended for Periel Aschenbrand, who is not invited to the dinner and drinks on June 19th. We apologize for this mistake, and for any inconvenience this may have caused you.

Please confirm receipt of this e-mail.

8

LIFE IS A DARING ADVENTURE OR NOTHING

Despite my suffering, I didn't regret a single second I had spent with Noam. I was a better person for having been with him—smarter, deeper, less reactionary, and more introspective. And Nico, for all of his flaws, had given me hope when I had none. It may have been misguided hope, but still it was hope. And for that I would forever be indebted.

Although we hadn't really resolved anything, Nico's birthday was coming up and I wanted to give him something special. He was difficult to shop for because he had everything he wanted and he certainly didn't *need* anything. He had beautiful homes filled with incredible art and books and curiosities from his travels around the world. But he had always been fond of vintage items and photography, and I had just unearthed an exposure meter from the 1930s that had belonged to my grandfather and I knew he would love it. I wrapped it beautifully, enclosed a seductive photo of myself, and wrote another mortifying letter that I should have burned instead of sending.

Nico,

I understand very little about the way technology works, but I've managed to glean that exposure meters have something to do with measuring light, which means, well, absolutely nothing to me. Shedding light, on the other hand, is quite another story. And while I'm sure you're just fine as far as equipment goes (in fact, I know you are) this belonged to my father's father, my grandfather Seymour, and I think it's pretty amazing.

Seymour, for better or for worse, did very little in the way of passing anything else down to me, nor, during the course of my life, did he shed light on anything in particular. But he sure had a lot of very cool stuff, which I've managed to snag, and that's good enough for me.

Given all that, I suppose one thing I did learn from him is that if we don't expect things from people that they are incapable of giving us, we are rarely disappointed. And disappointed is certainly no way to go through life. I don't really know much about else about Seymour, even though he only just died a few years ago.

It's entirely possible that Seymour was a fascinating individual—his things certainly seem to indicate as much. If you can learn about people from the things they accumulated through-out the course of their lives, it's possible that my grandfather was more interesting than I ever knew.

My impression is that my grandparents lived a very safe life. Helen Keller said: "Security is mostly a superstition. It does not exist in nature, nor do the children of men as a whole experience it. Avoiding danger is no safer in the long run than outright exposure. Life is either a daring adventure or nothing."

It's an interesting point.

Put that way, the thing to choose seems so fucking obvious.

I do remember once, when I was about five years old, visiting my grandparents, and convincing them to let me play on the swing set. I was swinging higher than I had ever swung before and was having an absolute blast. And then I fell off and I hurt my knee really badly. So badly, that to this day, I still have a scar.

So, maybe, in the end, I learned more than I thought. I learned I'm willing to fall and hurt my knee. I learned my knee will heal. Because if you want to soar, you have to be willing to fall . . .

Life is either a daring adventure or nothing, right?

Given that, in addition to everything else I've said, I'll say this, too:

I love you.

P

Soon after Nico's birthday, he invited me over for dinner. Nico could be really romantic when he felt like it and I was sure my letter had moved him and was absolutely certain that he was going to tell me that he had thought long and hard and was ready to really give us a chance. When I got there, primed and ready for him to profess his love to me, he told me that several other friends would be joining us and that we'd all be going out. I was expecting an intimate evening for two and he had planned a fucking dinner party.

This put me completely over the edge. Neither one of us was prepared for what came next but this was truly the straw that broke the camel's back. My reaction was completely out of left field, but I was so disappointed and felt like such a fool that I totally lost it.

I started screaming, at the tops of my lungs, "I am so sick of this shit. You invite me over for dinner and then you tell me that we're actually going out with six other people. I don't want to go out to dinner! One second you want to be with me and the next second you are totally unavailable. If that's how you want to be, you can find someone else to do that with, because *I'm not that girl!*"

Nico was in shock. And to be honest, I kind of surprised myself. I was not expecting to bug out like that and to be fair, Nico never said a word about an intimate evening or even alluded to anything of the sort. He had just asked me if I wanted to have dinner. We'd had dinner hundreds of times. He had given me no indication that tonight would be any different. Despite the fact that all evidence pointed to the contrary, I had convinced myself that Nico and I were destined to be together. I don't think he meant to drive me so crazy, but he definitely bit off more than he could chew. I certainly don't think he had any idea how fucking psycho I was going to get. I don't think I had any idea how psycho I was going to get either.

Because, of course, anyone who is actually *not* "that" girl does not need to *say* she is not that girl. Anyone who is *not* "that" girl *certainly* doesn't need to scream she is not that girl at the top of her lungs. Anyone who is screaming "I am not that girl" at the top of her lungs is screaming "that" because she obviously *is* that girl. She may not *want* to be "that" girl, but she is. I really never had been that girl before. I had turned into someone that I could not recognize and in screaming that, I think my brain was trying to remind the rest of me that once I had not been broken.

With that, I stormed out.

With the mail next day, I received a letter from the management company at Tishman Speyer. It read:

To whom it may concern,
Please be advised that it has come to our attention that Lil-

*lian Aschenbrand has passed away. Please be further advised that
the lease renewal that was to be offered to Ms. Lillian Aschenbrand is hereby revoked due to her death. If the apartment is not
surrendered, the Landlord intends to bring holdover proceedings
against the estate.*

*Should you wish to discuss this matter further, please contact
the office.*

Very truly yours,
Joseph Michael Lopez, Legal Affairs Unit

I immediately called good old Herbert Lust, attorney at law.
He said, "Sounds like it's time to start looking for new digs."

I had lived in almost every neighborhood in New York and knew
from experience that apartments are like everything else in the
city: it was possible to find something amazing, as long as you
were willing to hunt. My list of requirements was not as long as
it was specific. The apartment *had* to be a one bedroom; there
was no way I was moving into a studio. And it *had* to be below
Fourteenth Street. Ideally in Nolita. Unless you have millions
of dollars at your disposal, living in New York City is all about
compromise. Like most great things in life, you have to be willing to give something up to get something else. And I was willing to give up a lot if it kept me from moving into a shithole. I
proceeded to e-mail every single person I knew.

A few weeks later, after looking at approximately 4,836 apartments and reaching out to every single person I had ever met in
my life, a friend of a friend told me to call Bill Yen. I'd heard
Bill was a shady Chinese kid but my friend swore that if anyone
could find an apartment within my budget, it would be Bill (read:

Chinese Mafia). So I called him with my long list of requests. A few weeks later, Bill called me back and was like, "I have the perfect apartment for you. It's not on the market yet because it's in the middle of getting renovated, but if you're interested, you have to come see it today."

You'd think people were giving away the cure to cancer instead of letting you rent shitty, overpriced apartments. I was totally skeptical that Bill had the "perfect" apartment for me. To begin with, real estate agents are shady. I mean, they're pretty much one step above used-car salesmen. Real estate agents in *New York City* were some of the scummiest liars I had ever met. I didn't have any experience with real estate agents who may or may not have been affiliated with the Chinese Mafia, but I didn't have high hopes.

Bill met me on the corner of Mott and Broome, right at the border of Nolita, Chinatown, and Little Italy—and right around the corner from where I had lived with Noam. Bill had shaggy black hair and looked way more hipster than Mafia. He talked really slowly, like he was stoned, which he very well may have been. He nodded at me to indicate that I should follow him, which I did, down Mott Street for about a half a block. He stopped in front of a glass storefront with Chinese writing on it and a bunch of people who were alternately baking, screaming, and watching what looked like a Chinese soap opera. He smiled a toothy smile and said, "This is it."

I was like, "What do you mean, this is it? You want me to live in a bakery?"

You may think this is a joke, but believe me when I tell you that I had seen apartments with the shower stall *in* the kitchen— literally in the middle of the kitchen—so this was not outside the realm of possibility. Bill said, "No, dude. That's it."

He nodded his head toward a nondescript red metal door with graffiti all over it right next to the bakery. And when he opened it, there was a long, decrepit hallway filled with garbage bags and the scent of freshly baked goods mingled with rotting vegetables. The inside of the building was dingy and dark and literally looked straight out of a whorehouse from the 1970s.

I loved it.

And then I saw the stairs. And there was the compromise— the building had no elevator. Many years ago, I lived in a seven-floor walk-up and wanted to kill myself every single day. I was like, "Please don't tell me it's on the top floor."

Bill was like, "It's on the top floor, dude, but it's a great spot and it's gonna be brand-new."

By the time I reached the fifth floor, I was ready to collapse. "I guess I should be thankful it's only five flights, huh?"

Bill was like, "Dude, I live on an eighth-floor walk-up, but my rent is only eight hundred dollars a month, so, you know, whatevs. This is a great spot."

I hate it when people tell me how great things are when they are right in front of me. It's like I'm seeing the same exact thing you're seeing. I'll be the fucking judge of whether it's great or not, thank you very much. I walked into the apartment and there was soot and construction shit everywhere and like four Chinese men covered in white paint and dust crouched on the floor eating rice.

Bill was right. The apartment *was* being gutted. I couldn't believe it, everything was brand spanking new—wooden floor, the kitchen, the stove, the cabinets, the bathroom, the bathtub— everything. You could tell it had been a studio but they had put a wall up, so now it was a one bedroom. It was a small one bedroom, but still for little old me it was huge. It was in the right neighborhood, it was the right price, and I loved the apartment. But the stairs were a serious bitch. Bill said, "You should check out the roof, dude. No one ever goes up there, so it would be all yours and it's awesome."

Of course no one ever went up there. There were probably sixteen apartments in the whole building and I was more than certain that most of them were occupied by eighty-year-old Chinese people. I poked my head out the front door and walked up *another* set of stairs. I couldn't believe it. The roof was huge. And it had incredible, sweeping views of lower Manhattan. When I came back downstairs Bill was like, "Whaddaya think?"

I looked at Bill and his hipster haircut and his ripped-up denim jacket and his worn-out sneakers and his dumb beanie hat and I said, "I think it's awesome, *dude.*"

Bill gave me a big toothy grin and was like, "I told you it was a great spot. And the owner's pretty cool. The only thing to know is that the Chinese are like yellow Jews, so as long as you pay your rent on time, you're all good."

I handed Bill a deposit and made my way back to Grandma's. I had some serious packing to do.

When I got back to the apartment later that evening, I realized that nine months had passed since my grandmother's death, since Noam and I had broken up, and since my debacle with Nico had started. It didn't take a genius to know that this was my chance for a rebirth. I still hadn't had any real closure with Noam but at least I could say his name without bursting into tears, and I may have still been a little obsessed but I hadn't spoken to Nico in weeks. He had called me a bunch of times since my meltdown, but I didn't answer the phone and I deleted the messages without even listening to them. I hadn't even watched

Law and Order for almost two weeks. I was determined to come back to myself.

Hanna came over to help me gather the last odds and ends. The second she walked through the door I could tell something was off. I was like, "What's wrong?"

Hanna: "I'm panicking. I'm such a loser."

Me: "Will you stop saying that! You're *not* a loser. What happened now?"

Hanna: "It's Dan."

Me: "Oh God. Not him again."

I couldn't believe she hadn't gotten rid of this guy yet. The first time she went out with him—the *very first time*—he told her he had a girlfriend. And then he told her he *didn't* have a girlfriend. This enormous red flag was apparently not enough to make her realize that Dan was super sketchy. So she had sex with him and then she panicked that she had sex with him too soon. The sex part didn't concern me. What concerned me was that she slept at his house.

If you're having a one-night stand, don't linger around and snuggle and start getting delusional about the fact that you're having a one-night stand. If you're fucking some guy the first night you hang out with him, you damn well better be prepared for the fact that you are, most likely, having a one-night stand. And let's be very, very clear here. I don't think that you shouldn't have sex on the first date. I don't think there is anything wrong with having sex on the first date. What I *do* think is that if you're having sex on the first date, it should be because you want to have sex. *Not* because you have expectations for something else. Sex is not a promise for anything. It's not a promise for a phone call the next day; it's not a promise for breakfast; it's not even a promise for sex again. And I don't think there's anything wrong with that. In fact I think it's fantastic. But don't delude yourself into thinking it's something it's not.

When people show you who they are, you should believe them. If you don't, that's your problem. Dan revealed his deceptive nature almost immediately and Hanna chose to proceed with him anyway. She was upset early on, because she only heard from him once a week. This had been going on for a few months now. And every week she would call me and say, "I'm panicking."

And every week, I would ask, "Why are you panicking?"

And she would say, "I'm never going to hear from him again. I know I'm never going to hear from him again."

But of course he always wound up calling her and why wouldn't he? All he had to do was pick up the phone to get laid, and there she was. And while he did call her, it was hardly as often as she would have liked. And he continued to do things that upset her and yet she continued to hang out with him. For example, after a night of drinking and hanging out and having sex, he told her *not* to sleep over and she slept over anyway. Then he woke up super early the next morning and basically kicked her out of his apartment. This was about a week ago and she hadn't heard from him since, so now she was in panic mode. Again.

I was like, "Hanna, listen to me very carefully. I am telling you, from my experience with Nico, which is not identical but similar enough that it makes me want to throw up, that I would strongly advise you to pay close attention to what I am saying right now. This guy is *out*. O-U-T. Do you know what that means? It means that you are not to answer your phone if he calls you. It means that you should be dating other people, or better yet you shouldn't be dating at all. You're allowing this guy to treat you like shit, which is exactly *why* he is treating you like shit. You have to change your behavior. You can't change his behavior. You can only change your own. People treat you the way you allow them to."

As I was getting my last sentence out, Hanna received a text message from him. "Wanna meet up?"

Hanna looked at me. I was like, "Do not write back. You are not, under *any* circumstances allowed to write back."

Hanna glared at me. "What? Why not! I've been waiting for this text all week!"

I was like, "Honestly, are you fucking retarded? Have you not heard a word I said? It's a total booty call. If you're cool with that, then great, but you're obviously *not* cool with that. You don't want to be his booty call. You want to be his girlfriend."

"No," she's going, "he wants to see me. He wouldn't get in touch with me if he didn't want to see me. I think you're wrong."

I was like, "Hanna, trust me, I'm *not* wrong. Anyone who sends you a message at eleven o'clock at night after not having called you in a week is obviously under the impression that you're having casual sex. If you want to be having casual sex with him, then that's fine. But if what you're telling me is true, then you *don't* want to be having casual sex with him. And so the only thing you are doing is perpetuating his behavior."

Hanna glared at me. She said, "I think you're projecting. Are we talking about Nico or Dan?"

I went on, "Hanna, give me a break. This has nothing to do with Nico. Anyone who knows anything about the world knows that there are two reasons people get in touch with you at odd hours of the night: sex and drugs. So unless he's in the market for an eight ball, the only thing this guy is interested in is sex. If that's not okay with you, then *do not* write him back. It took him a week to get in touch with you and now that he has, it's almost midnight. And did he ask you how your week was? No. Did he ask you to see an art show with him? No. Did he ask you out to dinner next week? No. He wants to hang out with you and when does he want to hang out with you? Right now. It's the dictionary definition of a booty call."

Hanna, glaring at me again: "It's not midnight! It's eleven o'clock."

Me: "Jesus fucking Christ. Fine, it's eleven o'clock, whatever. It's closer to midnight than it is to any other time. Give me a break."

Hanna: "I really think he wants to see me."

Me: "Of course he wants to see you. Why wouldn't he want to see you? He has to *see* you in order to fuck you. He wants to fuck you. But that's *all* he wants from you. How do you not get that?"

I got up to go to the bathroom.

When I came back, Hanna was fiddling around with her phone. I was like, "What are you doing?"

Hanna: "Nothing."

Me: "You wrote him back, didn't you?"

Hanna: "Yes, but I told him I couldn't hang out tonight."

Me: "I can't believe you. I seriously cannot believe you."

Hanna, ballistic: "I told him I couldn't hang out! I did what you said! I told him I wasn't available!!"

I was like, "Hanna! Don't you understand that it doesn't matter *what* you told him. It doesn't matter that you told him you couldn't hang out! The fact that you texted him back means you *are* available. I don't know why you're asking me for advice if you're not going to take it."

I know that was kind of an unfair thing to say, but it was so fucking infuriating to sit there and watch her be so self-destructive. It was also, obviously, hitting way too close to home.

Hanna: "Why are you being so judgmental?"

Me: "I am *not* being judgmental. Okay. Maybe I am being a little bit judgmental. Maybe I'm judging myself. Either way, you're being really defensive!"

Hanna: "Well, I think you're wrong. I think I need to tell Dan that I *want* him to get in touch with me more often. How is he supposed to know that I want to talk to him more if I don't tell him?"

Me: "If someone wants to talk to you, they will call you. If you need to *tell* someone that you want them to call you, that is not a good sign. Haven't you read that book *He's Just Not That Into You*?"

Hanna, almost foaming at the mouth: "You're acting like you know what you would do if you were in my situation. You don't know what you would do if you were in my situation!"

My lapse in judgment with Nico notwithstanding, you can be shit fucking sure that I knew what I would do if I were in her situation. I knew *exactly* what I would do if I were in her situation. And beyond that, if I hadn't been emotionally ravaged, I wouldn't be in her situation. Obviously I had made some piss-poor decisions, but at least I had an excuse.

Hanna eventually left to go meet Dan. She actually *did* that. I was dumbstruck by her stupidity but I ultimately gave up. She was like, "Are you *sure* you don't mind if I go? He said he really wants to see me. And he sent me a smiley face."

I shook my head in despair. I actually felt sorry for her. At a certain point, there was really nothing else for me to say or do. She was a grown woman, after all. She was a moron, but she was a good kid, just a little bit misguided. She'd figure it out. I hoped.

Plus, I had bigger fish to fry. I had to get my ass in gear to move. As I was tossing out a few lamps and other odds and ends I had hidden from Uncle Bark, the phone rang. It was Roy. I said, "I'm so happy you called! I have big news! I found an apartment! And you're going to be so proud of me, I haven't even spoken to Nico in weeks!"

Roy: "Are you sitting down?"

Me, heart pounding: "Yeah, why?"

Roy: "Are you sitting on that disgusting plastic-covered couch?"

Me: "Fuck you. My couch is amazing."

Roy: "It's amazing for a nursing home."

Me: "Is this why you called me? To talk shit about my couch?"

Roy: "Merav is pregnant."

Me: "Holy shit."

Roy: "And we're getting married."

Me: "*Holy shit*. Are you serious?!"

I couldn't fucking believe it. I knew that after he returned from New York, they had started talking again, but I hadn't realized they got back together. I said, "What happened? You saw what a mess my life was and figured, 'Fuck it, maybe the grass isn't actually greener on the other side'?"

Roy: "Pretty much. Anyway, you better get your sorry ass here for the wedding. It's in three months."

Me: "Three months!? Oh my God. I can't believe this."

Roy: "Well believe it. And be there."

Me: "I promise you, I will definitely, definitely be there, no matter what. I'm ready for an adventure!"

9

EVERYTHING IS PERFECT

Moving day.

Because I had given Noam the vast majority of what we had gathered after a decade together, I had very little to be moved by way of furniture. He had moved into a bare apartment and needed furniture more than I did but beyond that, I hadn't really wanted any of it. It was too painful to look at it. And now I was pretty happy about it because I got to buy all new stuff and it was a lot easier to move when you hardly had anything *to* move. The only thing I was taking with me from grandmother's apartment was the pink couch, which was still covered in plastic. I just couldn't bear to part with it.

Upon hearing I was taking the couch, Uncle Bark, who had said in no uncertain terms that "anything you want is yours," started to hem and haw that now maybe he wanted it. I was like, "Uncle Bark, you live in a five-bedroom furnished home and you're constantly complaining that you have no room as it is. What in the world are you going to do with this couch?"

He relented. My mother, on the other hand, having seen my

new apartment, was less amenable to this idea. I brought her and my father over before I actually moved in to the apartment to show it to them. I thought they would be as excited as I was. My father, upon seeing the neighborhood, said, "Well, I guess you won't have a problem getting Chinese food."

My mother, upon entering the whorehouse-like hallway and seeing all the garbage bags lined up against the walls, was like, "Oh my God! Is it *legal* to store garbage here? This could be a real fire hazard."

Me: "Really, Mommy? How the fuck is this a fire hazard, exactly?"

My mother: "Peri, do you really need to use such language! It's dangerous to have so much garbage in the entrance of a building. Not to mention unsanitary."

Me: "Uh, Mommy, in case you haven't noticed, you're in *Chinatown*. The owners of this building are *Chinese*. Have you ever *been* to China? I have, and believe me, being sanitary isn't one of their strong points."

My mother: "Well, I think this is disgusting. I don't know how you're going to live like this." She turned to my father. "Michael, can you believe this? How is she going to live like this?"

My father ignored her. When my mother starts on one of her rants, my father usually ignores her. My father, of course, could have cared less either way. He was happy I wasn't doing anything "illegal" anymore and really just wanted the same thing he usually wanted—for me and my mother to shut up and stop arguing.

My mother went on, "Are there rats here? There could be an infestation of rats here, with all this garbage. How do you know there are no rats here? Peri, did you ask the landlord if there are rats in this building?"

I looked at my father for help. He looked back at me, as though to say, "I've got nothing for ya, kid."

Me: "Yeah, Mommy, right before I signed the lease, I asked Jonny if there were rats—"

My mother, interrupting me: "Your landlord's name is Jonny? I thought you said your landlord was Chinese."

Me: "He *is* Chinese!"

My mother, turning to my father: "Michael, have you ever heard of a Chinese man's name being Jonny? Why is his name Jonny?"

My father continued to ignore my mother. I, like a moron, engaged her.

Me: "I don't know why his name is Jonny! Why is your name Eve? Who gives a shit why his name is Jonny!"

This all really happened. My mother really asked these questions. My mother really asked questions like these *all the time* and actually expected answers. And she could just keep going on and on. No one else even needed to be in the room. She'd go on for hours.

My mother: "So he said there were no rats?"

Me: "No, Mommy, he told me the place was infested."

My mother: "I'm glad you think this is funny. Rats carry all sorts of horrible diseases."

My father, speaking for the first time: "Maybe they cook them in the bakery next door." And then he started cracking up.

After we got past the rats, my mother, who is an interior designer and thinks she is the only person in the entire world who knows anything about what furniture and apartments and houses should look like, went bananas when I told her I was taking Grandma's couch. She was like, "Oh, Peri, don't. It's so ugly."

Me: "It is *not* ugly! It's cool."

My mother: "Oh, yeah, very cool. Especially the plastic. That's my favorite part."

Me: "It just needs to be reupholstered."

My mother: "Oh, sure! I forgot how wealthy you are and that you know all about furniture! Do you have any idea how much it costs to reupholster a couch? And besides, that couch is going to look ridiculous in here. It's going to make the rest of the apartment look even more miniature than it does already!"

I can always count on my mother to say exactly what I don't want to hear. I thought the apartment was a relatively nice size. Granted it was the size of a very wealthy person's walk-in closet, but still.

I was like, "Thank you, Mommy, for all of your valuable input. I'm sure the couch will fit perfectly."

"And," my mother added, "I don't know how in the world you are going to manage with those stairs. They're insane."

The movers, upon arriving at my new den of iniquity, agreed with my mother. I could tell by the looks on their faces that they were less than pleased when they saw the stairs. They complained, but ultimately they brought all the boxes up the stairs pretty easily. The couch, on the other hand, was proving to be a bit of a problem. After about forty minutes of futzing with it, they gave up. One of them, the taller, bald one, Dennis, was like, "Sorry, lady."

I hate it when people call me "lady." I was like, "What do you mean, 'sorry'?"

Dennis: "It don't fit."

Me: "What do you mean, 'it don't fit'?"

Dennis shrugged his shoulders, like he couldn't have cared less, which was probably very much the case. He repeated, "The couch. It don't fit through the door."

Me: "Well, what do you propose to do about that?"

Dennis: "Ain't much I can do."

This incensed me. I was like, "I'm not sure what 'ain't much I can do' means. I'm pretty sure that you're not doing me a personal favor. I mean I'm fairly certain that your job—and by job, I mean, specifically what I hired to you to do, in fact, quite literally, what I am paying you to do—is to move my shit. I could shrug my shoulders my fucking self."

Dennis stared at me like I was a patient in a mental ward. I continued, "Couches are built to be *in* apartments, right?"

I waited for an answer to this rhetorical question.

Dennis: "Yeah, I guess."

Me: "So then the couch should fit through the door."

He pulled his tape measure out and shook it at me. "Maybe it *should* fit, but it don't fit. *You* got any ideas how to *make* it fit?"

With minor exception, most people are lazy. They don't want to do more than is absolutely necessary. And so, because almost everyone's first answer is almost always no as a general rule, I usually ignore people's first answer.

I looked at Dennis and started talking to him like a small child. "You're telling me that the couch doesn't fit because it's too wide to fit through the door, right?"

Dennis wasn't sure where I was going with this. He looked at me like, *That's what I just said, isn't it?* "Uh, yeah."

So I said, "Well, why don't you try taking the door off?"

Dennis started to say something but thought better of it.

I broke it down. I was like, "Listen, Dennis, I know that you're hot and you're tired and those stairs are a bitch, but you and I both know that no one is going anywhere until you get that couch into my apartment, so let's try to keep the bullshit to a minimum. The sooner you get it in, the sooner you get out of here."

I laid a hundred-dollar bill on the table.

Dennis walked into the hallway, where the other mover was standing with the couch. I don't know what he said to him but within fifteen minutes the couch miraculously made its way through the front door.

Suddenly, this couch, which moments earlier *didn't* fit into the apartment, was sitting in the middle of my living room. Suddenly, as quickly as the hundred dollars materialized, this couch, which moments earlier was too big, too wide, too whatever, to fit through the door, miraculously shrank, or the doorway became larger. It was like Moses parting the Red Sea. They didn't have to take the door off its hinges, or do anything but exert a tiny bit of fucking effort.

This couch, which had taken on all sorts of meaning in my life, was finally mine. It had so much history. My grandmother, who had it for more than half a century, thought it was so precious that she actually had the plastic cover custom-made for it. And then she spent so many years sitting in the same place that there was a spot in the corner where it was worn in the shape of her butt. This was the couch on which I had languished for nine long months, on which I had cried my eyes out and eaten boxes upon boxes of frozen pizza and watched hundreds, if not thousands, of episodes of *Law and Order: Special Victims Unit.*

This was the couch the fat, hairy Canadian Jew had ejaculated on. It was the couch on which I kissed Nico for the first time. And it was the couch on which I had laid as I nursed my heart and my soul back to emotional health. I had become so obsessed with this fucking couch that I had actually paid the movers an extra hundred dollars just so it could be part of my new life.

The moment had finally arrived.

Success!

I was triumphant, once again.

And God continued to have a wonderful sense of humor. While I was busy telling Dennis how to do his job, God was apparently kicked back on a cushy white cloud, laughing his ass off. The second the couch was actually *in* my apartment, the only thing I could think of was how I was going to get it out. It was a complete albatross. It looked like a normal-size couch at my grandmother's, because my grandmother lived in a normal-size apartment. My new apartment was miniscule, so it literally took up half the living room and looked like a piece of furniture from *Pee-wee's Playhouse* or *Alice in Wonderland*.

But I was too elated to care. That night I slept on a mattress on the floor in the bedroom. Because I didn't have curtains or blinds yet, I woke up at like five in the morning, sweltering hot. The sun was shining so brightly and the apartment was so small that the entire place was lit up. Even though I felt like I had sun blisters all over my face, I felt like a giant weight had been lifted from my shoulders. It suddenly occurred to me how unhealthy it had been for me to live at my grandmother's and for the first time in a very long time, I finally felt like me again.

A couple of short months later, I had managed to turn the apartment into an adorable little nest for myself. In creating a home, I had figuratively and literally rebuilt my life. Noam and I were on speaking terms but it was infrequent and while it was friendly, we were both very guarded. I had even seen Nico a couple of times for work and while I had been civil, I still kind of hated him. But mostly I was really happy about my new apartment and I was totally preoccupied with my upcoming trip to Israel. I hadn't been there in fifteen years and I was literally giddy with excitement. It felt like I was going home again.

All in all, things were looking up.

Even Hanna seemed to be pulling her shit together. She had finally gotten rid of Dan after she found an ad he had put online. She discovered that he didn't actually have a girlfriend. He had, like, ten. And, as it turned out, he was also a sex addict. Granted she found the ad while she was looking for a hookup herself but that's beside the point. Plus, she said, it was all in her past now. While I was packing for my trip to Israel she came over and told me she was planning a trip of her own. She said, "I think I'm going to go to India for a spiritual retreat. It's four hours of yoga a day and a one-hour lecture every evening. What do you think?"

Me: "I think it sounds like the best idea you have ever had."

Hanna: "My mother is going to kill me."

Me: "What do you mean, your mother is going to kill you?"

Hanna: "If I'm not actively searching for a husband, she thinks everything I do is a waste of time."

Spiritual enrichment, personal fulfillment—a waste of time? Brilliant. With a mother who says things like that, with a mother who thinks a trip to India is a *waste of time*, it's a miracle Hanna isn't *more* fucked-up than she is. It's no wonder she has some idiotic notion that the "perfect guy," a "nice Jewish boy," is lurking out there just waiting for her to find him. Her mother and all her coaches had brainwashed her to think that if she just looks hard enough, she's going to find him. I have told her time and time again that this is not how life works. Things rarely work out the way you expect them to. And thank fucking God.

Me, screaming: "Shakespeare, Hanna, Shakespeare! 'To thine own self be true!' For the love of God, for once go do something positive for yourself! Go to India."

Hanna: "I think I'm going to."

Me: "And another thing. I just wanted to thank you. You really helped me out of my hole and I really appreciate it. I think you're brilliant and wonderful and I'm sorry if I was harsh on you. And I love you."

As we said good-bye, she hugged me extra tight and said, "I hope you have an amazing time in Israel."

I winked at her on her way out and said, "I have every intention to."

10

GUY IS HERE

I really did have every intention of having an amazing time in Israel, and I was already off to a good start. One of my best friends worked for the airlines and had arranged a standby ticket for me. Some people hate flying standby, but I love it. I have always thrived on doing things last-minute and you can change standby tickets around at no charge whenever you want. I had booked my flight a few days in advance of the wedding so as to give myself a couple of days' wiggle room and this way I figured I'd be fine in case I got bumped off. I also loved flying standby because it was a fraction of the cost of a regular ticket *and* if you got lucky, you got to sit in first class. I was flying low season so I was pretty sure I was in good shape. Plus, I made sure to fly on a day that the plane looked relatively empty. Of course, one never really knew until the very last minute if you would make it on the flight and things could change from minute to minute, but I was okay with that. If there wasn't room and I got bumped, I'd just relist myself on the next flight. So while it was kind of a crapshoot, it was more than worth it and I'd never had a problem before.

As I had predicted, the flight went off without a hitch, and I was as happy as a pig in shit. I landed ten hours later and was greeted with love, affection, and a giant bottle of araq. Araq is the Middle Eastern version of pastis, which was suddenly my new favorite thing on the planet. It's anise-flavored liquor and you drink it straight, with lots of ice cubes. It tastes so good that you forget there's alcohol in it, which is obviously very dangerous. The party had officially begun. And it started the second I arrived.

It so happened that Talma and Yochanan, my surrogate parents, had just sold their house and with it, naturally, the garden that I had loved so very much as a child. My timing was impeccable. Had I not arrived when I did, I would never have seen that house again. In fact, had I not arrived when I did, many things wouldn't have happened. I wish I remembered more about the actual wedding but the only thing I know is that at the end of the night no one could find me. It would be Talma who finally discovered me sitting in the corner with a yarmulke on my head and tahini all over my face, devouring a giant pita filled with falafel.

The day *after* the wedding I was so hungover I wanted to die, but the festivities continued. The Israelis are a lively bunch. Because the political situation is so explosive and the threat of death is such a big part of their everyday lives, they really appreciate life for all it's worth. They're constantly drinking and smoking and laughing and eating and any cause is a cause to celebrate. Marriage, in particular, is a big deal. Israel may be the most modern country in the Middle East, but it's still traditional in many ways and it's extremely family and community-oriented and everyone is always together. Long term, this would probably make me want to put my face through a pane of glass. Short term, it was really fun.

The day after the wedding, we were at Talma and Yochanan's house in the kitchen, planning for another party there that night when Yochanan started screaming, "Where are my figs? Who took my figs?"

His twelve-year-old granddaughter, Mika, who was accustomed to his shenanigans, said, "I did."

Yochanan continued screaming, "Why did you take my figs! Who gave you permission to take my figs? Were they yours? Did they belong to you?"

Mika rolled her eyes and was like, "Whatever—they're *figs*."

In order for all this to make sense you have to understand some of the history here. When the Nazis invaded Bukovina, Yochanan was three years old. In order to save his life, his parents put him on a train headed to Palestine by way of Bucharest. They made him memorize a fake name for himself as well as for them and told him that if anyone ever asked, he was to say that his parents were dead. Unbeknownst to him, his father had sewn a piece of paper into the lining of his coat with his real name and address so if anyone found him, they might also find the paper and could safely return him to them.

The train—filled with two thousand children, many of whom who were sick and starving and dying of typhus—stopped in a place called Botoshan where there was a Jewish community and Jewish doctors. (Where there are Jews, there are doctors.) Yochanan, even in the face of such grim circumstances, was apparently so charming and so adorable that one of the doctors actually took him home. Yochanan lived with this doctor and his family for more than a year and the doctor eventually found the paper in the lining of his coat. Miraculously, his parents had survived the concentration camps and Yochanan was reunited with them.

Somehow that piece of paper survived and today, sixty-some-odd years later, it hangs above his desk in a frame.

Needless to say he had a crazy childhood and, as such, is excused for his insanity. And believe me that almost seven decades later there is some serious residual insanity. Exhibit A: The fig story. Also, as a Holocaust survivor, he categorically *refuses* to throw away food. In fact, right after he flipped out over the figs, he tried to feed me a rotten olive. When I protested, he started screaming, "Olives cannot be rotten!"

And then he shoved it in my mouth. I think he was right because even though there was a moldy film on the juice the olives were sitting in, the olive tasted fine. When he forced me to admit there was nothing wrong with the olive, I was like, "But still, who wants to eat a moldy olive?"

Yochanan screamed, "There is no such thing as a moldy olive!"

Understandably, Yochanan has a different relationship with food than the rest of us because the rest of us were never starved nearly to death. He is constantly cooking obscene amounts of food and hoarding things in jars and cupboards and if he catches you trying to throw something out, he goes completely ballistic. You are also never *ever* allowed to say food is disgusting. This is grounds for him to go completely ape-shit crazy. So these are the things we have to tolerate. He can be totally impossible but he's been through so much and he's so much fun and so brilliant and lovable that it's really kind of easy to overlook his insanity. Plus, he's really funny.

For example, after the olive incident he had a huge fight with Talma for throwing out six rotten tomatoes. I was sitting in the garden, which was adjacent to the kitchen, and he sat down next to me with the bag of rotten tomatoes that he'd rescued from the garbage and said, "I think I am going to get separated. I'm much too busy for this aggravation. I have many interests—in art, in literature . . . And I have many friends, as well. I simply don't have time for this."

Unbeknownst to Yochanan, Talma was standing right behind him and obviously heard everything he said. She was like, "Really? You know where the door is, Yochanan. *Please* go."

Yochanan, with a shit-eating grin, didn't skip a beat. He said to me, "You know what the problem is? The problem is that in the past few years, she has become very assertive. She wasn't like this before."

Talma met Yochanan when she was sixteen years old. Yochanan was a couple of years older and used to race up to her on his bicycle and unzip her sweatshirt and race away. Shortly thereafter, she lost her virginity to him in a bomb shelter. Other than the fact that Yochanan fought in three wars, they hadn't left each other's sides since. They were both in their late sixties now. The mere thought that he could survive one day without her was laughable.

In fact, I was laughing so hard and was so amused by all this, I didn't even realize that the garden had started to fill up with people and was buzzing with activity. All these people had arrived and they were eating and drinking and laughing and then I heard somebody scream, "Guy is here!"

Inexplicably, I suddenly felt like I was having a full-blown out-of-body experience. I had no idea who Guy was. I had never even heard his name before. But the second I heard his name—I swear to God—I actually felt the earth move. Maybe on some subconscious level I thought of Lori's brother, Guy, who had been killed on 9/11. I honestly don't know. But I had never experienced anything like that before in my entire life.

And then I saw him.

And all bets were off.

He was literally the most beautiful human being I had ever seen. He had smooth, mocha skin and jet-black hair, speckled with silver. He had crazy long black eyelashes and dark-brown eyes that were deep and soulful with just the slightest hint of a twinkle to let you know that he was more than just a pretty face. He had that sexy I-haven't-shaved-in-a-couple-of-days scruff and I liked his teeth. Most people in the Middle East—most people in the world, including certain dentists incidentally— have heinous teeth that are brown and crooked and rotting out of their heads. Guy's teeth were not perfect, but they were almost perfect. He was tall but not too tall and I could tell he had a sick body. He was muscular the way a runner or soccer player is muscular. And he had a great ass. And while there was something gentle and shy about him, there was also something confident and incredibly sexy. He was seriously drop-dead gorgeous and I could not stop staring at him. He kept catching me staring at him, which was mildly embarrassing but it also meant he was staring at me. I decided right then and there that I needed to have my way with him.

I excused myself from the table, did some quick investigating, and discerned that Guy was one of Roy's best friends and I had apparently met him at the wedding. It was a testament to how drunk I was that I didn't even remember. When I returned, Guy sat down at the same table Talma and Yochanan were sitting at and Roy joined us. We were having a fairly inane conversation that I wasn't paying attention to because I was fantasizing about tearing Guy's clothes off when Roy said something about how Guy was a really good cook and that he was particularly gifted when it came to fish. Yochanan started shouting, "I am a great chef!"

And then he started telling Guy that Guy may think he knows how to cook fish but Yochanan could teach him the *real* way to cook fish, the *best* way to cook fish and on and on it went. Guy, for his part, took all this quite well. Had I walked into someone's home and been greeted by such a raving lunatic, I'm not sure how I would have reacted. It's not like Guy knew Yochanan. It's not like he had ever met him before. It's not like a strange man wasn't lecturing him on something he obviously knew a great deal about. But he took it. And he didn't take it the way most people take it. He took it—differently. He was so laid-back and chill. He was like, *You are obviously a fucking lunatic and that's fine but if you want to cook me a fish dinner so you can prove to me that you know how to cook fish better than I do, or so you can prove to me that you can cook salmon and I'm going to think it's trout, I'll be more than happy to come over for dinner.*

There are few things sexier than a man who has nothing to prove. I was so turned on that I would have seriously had sex with him right then and there. But Guy was really kind of shy and we didn't say more than a few words to each other that day.

A few nights later I went out with Roy and a bunch of his friends to a bar in Tel Aviv. Keeping in mind the year I just had, the fact that Roy had just gotten married and had a pregnant wife at home, and how infrequently we saw each other, it was a big deal to be let out like this. And I, for one, had every intention of making the most of it.

The bar was crowded and dark and smoky and people were dancing on the tables and soon I was one of them. I was having the time of my life. At some point, this guy named Sammy started hitting on me relentlessly. He was kind of ridiculous, with his wife beater and his gold chain. He was almost a caricature of himself but I thought he was sort of hot in a cheesy macho kind of way. Plus, he was mildly entertaining, so I played along. After about fifteen minutes of this, out of the corner of my eye, I saw Guy walk in. I was like, *See ya later, Sammy. My night is about to get interesting.* Guy sat down at the bar and I sashayed my little ass over and sat down right next to him.

He was even sexier than I remembered.

As it turned out, he was also painfully boring.

I could not have been more straightforward in my intentions had I dropped to my knees in the middle of the bar. I mean, as far as I was concerned, I was making it pretty clear that I was interested in him. In fact, until he opened his mouth, I was pretty much ready to leave the bar with him that instant. But for some reason he wouldn't stop talking about parking. He droned on and on about how it had taken him forever to find a parking spot and how the parking situation in Tel Aviv was so terrible and on he went until I finally couldn't take it anymore. I was so bored and underwhelmed that after about twenty minutes of this I actually got up and walked away. As luck would have it, I found Sammy, who was standing pretty much exactly where I'd left him and was thrilled to see me. We walked outside, sat down on a bench, and proceeded to make out for what I thought was about half an hour.

Next thing I know it's two o'clock in the morning and I am wasted, sitting on a bench in a foreign country with some guy I just met who is trying to convince me to come home with him. If Sammy looked ridiculous after several drinks in the dark lighting of the bar, now that I was more sober and essentially sitting under a streetlight I wanted to die. My araq-induced stupor and my excitement over being at a tacky bar in Tel Aviv led me to believe that Sammy was hot, when he was in fact *not* hot at all. Sammy, as it turned out, was the very opposite of hot. He was the kind of guy you *think* is hot when you're wasted and in a dark bar in a foreign country—contextually hot, as it were. Had I found him in New York City, it would have been in some cheesy club in the Meatpacking District and he would have been from New Jersey. Or worse, Staten Island. I could try to make this sound better than it actually was, but if I'm really going to be honest, I had just made out with a character out of a Sacha Baron Cohen skit.

Upon realizing this dreadful error and having no interest in repeating my ordeal with the masturbating Canadian, I found Roy and got the hell out of there.

So that was that.

I spent seven more glorious days with Roy and Talma and Yochanan and the rest of my family. We cooked meals and went to the beach and went to Jerusalem and the Dead Sea and traveled around and I fell in love with the country all over again. A week later, when it was time to return, I went to the airport firm in my conviction that I would return sooner rather than later, even if it killed me. I knew there was a very real possibility that it *would* actually kill me, given all the suicide bombings and other insanity that took place in that neck of the woods.

It's worth noting that even I, the most paranoid of paranoid, have to admit that the American media's version of what goes on in Israel is totally sensationalized and wildly inaccurate. Having not been in Israel for fifteen years, I was mildly concerned for my safety after everything I had seen on television. But being in Tel Aviv is akin to being on the Upper West Side of New York City during Hurricane Sandy. It's like you know something super fucked-up is going on but it's not *really* affecting *your* life. Which is part of the problem, of course, but that's not the point. The point is that I was safely on my way home, feeling vibrant and rejuvenated, vowing to return as soon as humanly possible.

As I was in line waiting to check in at the airport, I was waxing nostalgic, thinking about how insane it was that I had suffered for so long over Nico and Noam and about how good I felt now. I was thinking about how incredible it had been to see everyone and how lucky I was. I was thinking about how nice it had been to be out of New York, even though I loved New York, and how incredible it was to reconnect with my family and my roots. I was thinking about how much I loved the weather and the flowers in Israel and how wonderful I felt. I was thinking about all of these things as I presented my passport to the man behind the counter. I told him I was flying standby and asked him to check my status. The man said that there was plenty of room on the plane and I was free to check in.

So I checked my luggage and made my way through security and passport control. If you think the security is annoying in America, try getting in and out of Israel. It's like a police interrogation: Who are you? Where are you from? What were you doing in Israel? Has anybody given you anything to take out of the country? If so, it could be a bomb. Do you know that Arabs can't be trusted? How many times a day do you shit? They are not fucking around over there. It took more than an hour to get to my gate.

The thing about flying standby is that like most things that are superfantastic, there is a downside. Even though *I* felt like a movie star flying first-class, the people who work for the airline knew I was just a lowly second-class citizen flying on the goodwill of an employee. And because you are essentially a nonrevenue customer, you have to wait for every single other passenger to board the plane before they let you on. Once you're on the plane, you're golden, but I wasn't on the plane yet. I was, quite literally, steps away from walking on when a man with crooked brown teeth, beady eyes, and a long, greasy ponytail, said to me, "Zis flight iz foole."

It took me a moment to decipher what he was saying, which was, "This flight is full."

I was like, "You have to be kidding me!"

Beady Eyes repeated himself as though I hadn't heard him properly the first time, "Zis flight iz foole."

I said, "But that's impossible. They told me when I checked in that there was definitely room. And they've given me a ticket."

In America, where the customer is always right, this may have made an impression on someone. But Israelis seriously just don't give a fuck. Beady Eyes repeated "it's foole" again and just as I was about to reply, he straight up walked away from me. It took me about ten minutes to discern that the flight was not actually "foole," but it was "overweight" and, as such, they were not letting anyone else on the plane. Who had ever even heard of such a thing?

I couldn't believe my luck. I had been flying standby for years and nothing like this had ever happened and there wasn't anything I could do. The next available flight that looked like it had room wasn't until the day after next. I reminded myself that I had known from the beginning that this might happen and I figured that as long as there wasn't a war going on, there were worse things than being stuck in Tel Aviv. I went to find my luggage, relisted myself on a flight back to New York, and after running around from one side of the terminal to the other like a chicken with my head cut off, I resigned myself to an extra two days in the Holy Land.

I was finally about to exit the airport when something very strange occurred. A female security guard—dressed in full military gear, complete with a machine gun strapped across her chest—

stopped me. To this day, I have no idea why she stopped me, but she did. She said, "Didn't you just get here a few hours ago?"

I was like, "Uhhhh, yes."

She said, "Well, then why are you leaving?"

Let's be clear here. Israel may be a tiny country but Ben Gurion is a major international airport. There are tens of thousands of people who come and go from that airport every day. I have no idea how or why she remembered me and, somewhat baffled, I told her the standby story and how I had gotten kicked off the flight because it was overweight.

She gave me a once-over and very matter-of-factly said, "Well, God obviously has other plans for you. He's not ready for you to leave Israel yet."

It was a very intense and very strange interaction. I'm like the least religious person in the world. I mean, I'm practically an anarchist but even I was taken aback by this.

And then I put the thought out of my head and called Roy.

Even though it was two in the morning, like a good surrogate brother he offered to come collect me from the airport. Like an idiot I told him I would take a taxi. I had no money and I had no phone: in a fit of drunken idiotic joy, some fat, hairy Middle Easterner had tossed my Chanel bag and with it my iPhone into the pool at Roy's wedding—and I should have known better than to turn down Roy's offer. But I didn't know better. Instead, as though I were in New York City, I hailed a taxi and climbed in.

And as soon as I got in the cab, it hit me that it was the middle of the night and I was in a country that I didn't really know. Ultimately, even though I spoke the language, I was a foreigner. Moreover, I was stuck in this taxi with no phone, a man who looked like an Arab, and no idea where I was going. I became completely convinced that he was kidnapping me and bringing me to who-the-fuck-knows-where. I could already see images of myself on YouTube, holding an Arabic newspaper with the current date and time, with my head being chopped off.

Suffice it to say I was *bugging out*.

We were on the highway and I began to formulate a plan as to how I was going to jump out of the taxi. *How would I survive such a jump*, I wondered. And then I started to notice the signs along the side of the highway and I realized that we were not headed toward Tel Aviv. I began to have a full-blown panic attack, in earnest. I was sweating and starting to hyperventilate. In the calmest voice I could muster, I said, "It doesn't look like we're heading toward Tel Aviv."

Not that I knew what the fuck I was talking about or where Tel Aviv was in relation to anything else in Israel, but I was convinced we were going the wrong way and that my life was in imminent danger.

In a very ominous voice (or in a voice I thought was very ominous), the taxi driver said, "Why would we be headed toward Tel Aviv?"

Why, indeed, would we be headed toward Tel Aviv? Roy didn't live in Tel Aviv. He lived right outside of Tel Aviv and actually, coming from the airport, it was in a completely different direction than Tel Aviv. But I had no idea where I was or where we were going and it literally took every fiber of my being to convince myself that my driver was not a mujahideen. After what felt like a lifetime, we finally pulled up in front of Roy's house and he was downstairs waiting for me to help with my suitcases and to pay the taxi driver. As the taxi drove away, Roy realized that I was shaking and all fucked-up and totally hysterical. He was like, "What's wrong with you?"

I told him the whole story about how I didn't know where we were going and I didn't have a phone and I thought I was getting kidnapped. By the time I got to the end, we were back in his apartment and he was laughing so hard he could hardly breathe. When he finally caught his breath, he started screaming, "You're an idiot! You are *such* an idiot! You are literally the dumbest person on earth! Your taxi driver wasn't even Arab!"

Me: "What do you mean, he wasn't Arab?"

Roy: "No, he wasn't Arab! He was Russian! From Georgia!"

Me: "How the fuck am I supposed to know the difference! I'd like to see you come to New York and discern between someone from the Dominican Republic and Puerto Rico!"

Roy: "You're no smarter than a barnyard animal. Drink this," he said, as he handed me a glass of araq. "And go to sleep, we have a big day tomorrow."

11

PLEASE DON'T GO

The second I woke up the next morning Roy started in on me. I was still reeling from all the drama the night before but he was having none of it. When I finally dragged myself into the living room, Roy barely looked up. He said, "You better get your pathetic self ready. We're going out tonight."

I was like, "I honestly don't think I can take any more excitement."

Roy, like me, doesn't take no very well as an answer. He said, "It's your last night. *We're going out.*"

I thought for a moment and said, "Fine. Then call Guy and tell him to come with us."

Roy raised his eyebrow at me the way only someone who has known you your entire life can raise their eyebrow at you. He didn't have to say a word and yet I knew exactly what he was asking me, which was, *What are you up to?*

I raised my eyebrow back at him and he understood exactly what I was telling him, too, which was, *Just do it.*

I didn't know what was going on with Roy, but I could tell he wanted to get his party on and I certainly wasn't going to try to stop him. In the meantime, we had a whole day to kill, so reverting back to our childhood antics we devised a plan to scare the shit out of his parents who were under the impression that I was already back in New York.

Roy walked into his parents' kitchen and told Talma there was a package at the door and the postman was waiting for her to sign for it. Suspecting nothing, she walked over to the door and of course started yelling to Roy that no one was there, at which point I jumped out from behind a bush and, like a six-year-old, screamed, "Surprise!!! I'm back!"

Talma got so scared she started screaming herself. Upon hearing all this commotion, Yochanan came running out of the pantry, where he hoards all his food, and began hollering, "Tell me something, what is wrong with you? You are all interrupting me from my work! Can't everyone see I'm working? Are you mentally retarded?"

We may have been retarded but Yochanan had plunged well off the deep end. The "work" that we had "interrupted" was him making soup with his "new recipe" out of potato skins.

Cut to later that night:

I was in line with Roy and a few of his friends waiting to get into some club in Tel Aviv and I was less than impressed. To begin with, I don't like waiting in line for anything. *Ever.* I waited in lines to get into the Limelight when it was the coolest night-club on the planet—when I was *sixteen.* So waiting in line to get into some shithole club in the Middle East at age thirty-three was not my idea of a good time. Suddenly Guy shows up. He walks right up to me, looks me up and down, and says, "You look great."

I very uncharacteristically felt my face go red.

The club was deafeningly loud and completely packed. We

were standing near a speaker and I felt like my eardrum was about to blow out and it was so crowded you could hardly move. I shouted, "Can we please get the fuck out of here?"

Guy took my hand and led me to the exit and everyone else we were with followed suit. I thought, *Finally some assertiveness.* When we got outside, he just shook his head and said, "That was pathetic."

I liked that he was willing to leave the club just because I wanted to but I also liked that he knew it was lame. I started to think he was sexy again and by the time we arrived at our next destination, I basically had one goal, which was to have sex with Guy that night. I figured if all went well, I would go home with him that night, get back to Roy's to finish packing, and still have enough time to spend a couple of quality hours on the beach before I went to the airport. The bar was much more intimate than the club so that was good, and Guy was *finally* talking to me but he was still pretty shy, which was grating on my nerves. I was on the clock, after all. I had a flight in twelve hours and had absolutely no qualms about having a quickie in the bar bathroom.

After a couple of hours, though, it was painfully obvious that nothing was happening and just as I started to lose my patience with him, someone accidentally knocked over a barstool. It landed right on his big toe, which promptly turned blue. I could tell he was in a lot of pain and I ran over to the bar to get him some ice. After I inspected his toe to make sure it didn't need to be amputated, I went back to the bar, ordered another drink, and thought to myself, *This is fucking ridiculous. How hard do I have to work to get into this guy's pants?*

Apparently, my Nurse Betty act was effective because next thing I knew Guy was standing right next to me. And when I say right next to me, I mean he was practically on top of me. He shifted around a little bit before he said, "You should come over tomorrow night and let me cook you dinner."

I stared at him, which seemed to make him nervous because he started to backtrack and said, "Or, if you want, you and um, Roy can come over. Or, um, you know, just you."

I looked at him dead in the eyes and said, "I'm supposed to get on a plane tomorrow night. Is it really worth it to stay in Israel just to have *dinner* with you?"

Guy returned my stare and said, "You're a big girl. You can make that decision by yourself."

I liked that answer. Most men are intimidated by me, which is so boring I can hardly begin to tell you. I respected a man who could spar with me. I said, "I *know* I'm a big girl and I can make that decision by myself. But that wasn't the question. The question was: Is it really worth it to stay in this country just to have *dinner* with you?"

Without flinching, Guy said, "Clearly."

I liked *that* answer even more.

I figured, all things being equal, really, what did I have to lose?

Roy drove Guy home and when he got out of the car, he gave me a kiss on the cheek and it took everything in my power not to behave like a complete whore and just take my underwear off and follow him up to his apartment.

I spent the better part of the next day packing and trying to figure out what underwear to wear and whether to wear a bra for my rendezvous with Guy later that evening. I finally decided on a pair of black lace underwear and a matching bra.

Then I took a shower. This may seem very straightforward but it's not. Taking a shower in Israel, which is essentially in the middle of the desert and where water is precious and scarce, is different than taking a shower in America. Taking a shower in Israel entails flipping a switch and heating the water, which comes from a tank, then you have to wait for the water to heat up and the whole thing is a fucking procedure. The rule is to use as little water as you can and get in and out as quickly as humanly possible. This was particularly challenging because I was trying to shave not only my legs, my armpits, and my bikini line but also inside my ass, which is a delicate operation as one may well imagine. I understand that many women in the postindustrialized West *wax* this part of their body but I can't do that because I get terrible ingrown hairs and rashes and then my asshole itches for weeks, and it just doesn't work. And I haven't ever had laser so I don't know anything about that. What I do know is that when I shave the inside of my ass, I have to bend over and put my head in between my legs like how a cat licks its own genitals to make sure I get a clean shave while simultaneously making sure not to slice off my anus.

It took forever in the confines of Roy's small shower and with the shitty water pressure but I was finally satisfied. I got out of the shower, pranced around in front of the mirror a little bit, and thought, *You are one sexy bitch.*

It occured me as I was putting my makeup on in the bathroom of Roy's house about an hour before Guy was meant to come pick me up that I had butterflies in my stomach. I realized I was going on my first *real* date in ten years.

I was so nervous that I threw up.

Guy, for his part, didn't seem nervous at all. He smelled delicious and he looked adorable enough to eat alive. Israel may be very sophisticated in terms of weaponry, excellent food, and great wine, but they are about fifteen years behind New York in terms of fashion and style. I'm terribly snotty when it comes to clothes, but even I had to admit that his outfit was pretty cute. He was wearing a black T-shirt, Levi's, and Pumas. It wasn't the height of avant-garde fashion but it worked.

His apartment, on the other hand, was another story entirely. It was very clean, so that was a good thing. But that was pretty much the only good thing. There was the couch, which should have been set on fire, but that was nothing compared to the terrible excuse for a painting that was hanging above the couch. Then there was a whole bunch of trinkets that I had to control myself not to put in the trash. In short order, pretty much everything in the apartment needed to go directly into the garbage. But instead of dismissing him for it, for some strange reason, I thought, *These are all things that can be changed.* I'm generally much less forgiving in these areas, but I reminded myself that I didn't come to redecorate. I came to get laid.

And because I came to get laid, I wasn't actually expecting to eat dinner. Which is to say that I was not only astonished but also mildly horrified to discover that not only had Guy actually cooked dinner, but he had prepared a five-course gourmet meal. Every time I thought we were done eating, he brought another dish: skewered shrimp, couscous, fresh figs stuffed with Roquefort cheese, grilled eggplant, red snapper. It was like the last fucking supper.

Don't get me wrong. I was thoroughly impressed with his cooking skills and I ate like a pig. But I live in Manhattan, where there are plenty of good restaurants. And although I gorged myself, I had not rearranged my travel plans for a bowl of hummus.

This is what I was thinking as I brought dishes to the kitchen when Guy said to me, "You know what?"

And I was like, "What?"

And he said, "You're really pretty."

I was like, "Thank you."

And he goes, "No, I mean you're really, *really* pretty."

And then, out of absolutely nowhere, he kissed me.

It was the craziest, most intense kiss I had ever experienced in my life. The room was spinning. I felt like I was in a k-hole or ODing on ecstasy. I mean it was so fucking crazy I couldn't tell if I was just really horny or if I just peed in my pants. (Luckily it turned out to be the former.)

That night, we had what I can only describe as seriously the most incredible sex I have ever had in my life. Dude knew how to fuck. I mean, listen, some guys have no idea how to fuck and some guys know how to fuck and then *some* guys really know how to *fuck*. And Guy fell into the last category. And let's be clear here. I'd been around the block a few times (more than a few times, really) and even though my recent track record was kind of spotty, I'd had my fair share of great lovers. Or at least I thought I had. I didn't even know you could have sex like this.

It was so good that in a totally unprecedented move I broke my cardinal rule and instead of bolting I spent the night. I have never been big on sleepovers with people I just met. Sex is one thing. Waking up next to a stranger with bad breath is quite another story. And even though I couldn't help feeling like I was on borrowed time, I felt oddly calm. Or perhaps I felt oddly calm precisely *because* I felt like I was on borrowed time. Normally I would have been in and out of there as fast as humanly possible so as not to form any irrational bonds with a virtual stranger. Just because we're fucking doesn't mean we're friends and I'm not big on formalities. But all my rules seemed to have gone straight out the window with Guy.

Instead of bailing, the next morning I went to brunch with him. If that weren't bad enough, we went to this ridiculously romantic restaurant overlooking the sea. This was completely out of character for me. I go to brunch with Hanna and Uncle Bark, not with men I pick up in bars. Beyond that, instead of packing, which is what I should have been doing, I was drinking fresh-squeezed orange juice while staring out at the Mediterranean. I was totally lost in my thoughts when Guy jolted me back to reality: "We should figure something out."

I was like, "What do you mean?"

He said, "You know, between Tel Aviv and New York."

Whoa. As I was thinking, *He has obviously lost his mind.* A man with two hearing aids came up to our table trying to hawk us his wares. He had a bunch of gadgets and trinkets—pens, key chains, magnets—and I shook my head to communicate, "Thanks, but no thanks. The fact that you can't hear is not going to manipulate me into buying a tchotchke from you."

Israelis are generally a pushy bunch and, apparently, deaf Israelis were no exception. He put a magnet on our table despite my protests. I was about to mouth no, but Guy gave him a few shekels and picked up the magnet and placed it in front of me.

On it was a drawing of a hand, configured in American Sign Language. The shape of which was almost a *W.* Above the hand, something was written in Hebrew. Below the hand, something was written in English. While my spoken Hebrew is pretty good, my reading skills aren't so hot, so I wasn't sure that I had read what I thought I had read. My eyes darted to the bottom of the magnet, where there was no possible way to misread what was written in American English. It said, I LOVE YOU.

I love you?

I love you?

I didn't dare say a word, but what I was thinking was, *Dude is bugging.*

Back in the car, on the way back to his place, Guy started singing KC and the Sunshine Band's "Please Don't Go" in his hilarious accent. I was laughing but when we pulled up to his building, he stopped and with his body he pushed my body up against the wall and looked at me in a way that felt like his eyes were about to bore a hole straight through my head. He said, "I haven't felt like this in a very, very long time. Seriously. Stay. Stay one more day."

My head started spinning and I didn't know what was going on. All the hormones and adrenaline and I don't know—the whole thing was just so fucking crazy. I wasn't even supposed to *be* in Israel let alone getting laid, never mind getting caught up in some love affair. If anything, I had planned for a casual one-night stand—a plan that had clearly gone terribly awry.

In the end, the decision seemed so obvious. I figured, *What's one more day?*

And I stayed.

Loathe as I was to admit it, it did feel like there was really something there, even beyond the mind-blowing sex. And since none of this actually felt real, I was completely uninhibited, without a care in the world. Being with Guy was so easy—granted almost everything is easy when you're on vacation—but it was more than that. We had just met but I felt like I had known him my entire life. There was something about being with him that made me feel very at home. Part of it, I think, had to do with the fact that he was Israeli and that although we were culturally very different I felt connected to him. I couldn't really explain or understand it, but I also trusted him implicitly. I was completely and totally myself. And he was in complete and total awe of me.

I told him about my life in New York and what I did and all the places I had lived and about Noam and why we broke up and it was pretty clear that he thought I was out of my fucking mind and also he'd never come across anyone like me in his entire life. I was a total novelty. It was totally obvious he adored me.

And I liked him, too. I mean the last thing I was looking for was a boyfriend, let alone one who lived on another continent, but he was starting to grow on me. He was the perfect combination of gentle and tough. He was really funny and he was really smart. And very fucking sexy.

In between fucking and eating, we went to the beach. Everything looks good when you're in the Mediterranean Sea but while I was standing with Guy in the water, with his arms around me, I was literally in bliss. Just for that very moment, I knew that if I never saw Guy again (and I pretty much figured I wouldn't) all of my suffering over the past year had been worth it. Looking out into the infiniteness of the water, it was almost inconceivable to think that life could be so painful and so blissful all at once.

And just like that it was twenty-four hours later and it was time to say good-bye, for real. A gentleman until the end, Guy drove me to the airport, where we had a tearful parting. At least I was tearful. Guy was stoic, exhibiting the typically tough exterior of the Israeli male. Years of war and death and violence and living in a place where at any moment someone could detonate himself does that to people I imagined.

And although he didn't say much, his silence spoke volumes. Plus, the trademark twinkle in his eyes was all but gone. I was trying to keep it together but I was really kind of a mess. I attempted to compose myself as I handed the woman behind the counter my passport and my ticket. She looked at my passport, looked at me, and looked back down at my passport. Then she looked at my ticket and looked at me—and started laughing. I was in no mood for games. I was like, "Is there something funny that I'm missing? Why are you laughing?"

She could tell I was genuinely upset and she softened and said, "I'm laughing because your ticket is a standby ticket and the day after tomorrow is Yom Kippur! The flight today is over-booked by twenty people and so is every other flight for the next seven days."

Now I started to laugh. I was like, "You're kidding, right?"

She stopped laughing and said, "Why would I be kidding?"

Apparently, traveling to and from Israel around Yom Kippur, the holiest day of the Jewish year, was akin to traveling during Thanksgiving, Christmas, or New Year's. In other words, no, she wasn't kidding and yes, I was stuck, for lack of a better word, again, in Tel Aviv for at least another week.

Guy, upon hearing this, immediately perked up. The sparkle returned to his eyes and he had a huge grin on his face. He picked me up, kissed me, spun me around, and said, "This is excellent."

For the next seven days, I had absolutely nothing at stake, nothing to lose, nothing to fear, nothing to even think about other than the fact that I was enjoying every single moment of my existence for the first time in I couldn't even remember how long. I basically spent the next week half-naked, drinking, smoking, and fucking my brains out. I was having the time of my life.

But as we all know, all good things must come to an end. Alternately, as the great poet T. S. Eliot pointed out, "The end is where we start from."

Part III

12

THE N FROM N-I-C-E

A few weeks after I returned to New York City, I was sitting on my (still enormous-looking) pink couch, *sans* plastic cover. It was a testament to my mental health that I had finally removed the plastic cover. It was also much more comfortable this way. So I was lounging on the couch, talking to Guy on the phone about his impending visit in a couple months. After our weeklong romance, we had decided that he would come visit me and I was really excited. I was like, "I really can't wait to see you."

To which he replied, "Me too. By the way, I've decided I'm not going to have sex with anyone else until I see you."

That caught me off guard. "You did? Why?"

Guy said, "I think I'm in love with you."

I started stammering and stuttering. He started laughing and interrupted me. "Relax. I said I *think* I'm in love with you. I didn't say I was sure."

When we got off the phone, I started pacing around my apartment. *In love with me?* How could he be in love with me? I mean, I was definitely kind of crazy about him, but *in love*? We'd spent all of eight days together. Certainly he was having some sort of delusion. The week we spent together had been magical but it was, well, a week. The I LOVE YOU magnet he gave me was on my refrigerator but that didn't freak me out anymore. I had rationalized that giving someone a *magnet* is totally different than *saying*, "I love you."

As I was processing all this, I walked over to my window and stared blankly at the street below. I don't know why I walked over to the window. There was no reason to. I could have just as easily continued pacing. But I walked over to the window and was just sort of absentmindedly staring when I suddenly saw Noam. For a second, I literally thought I was hallucinating. I had looked out this window thousands of times and I had never, ever seen *anyone* I knew. I started to open the window and was about to scream his name. I had no idea what I would even say. I hadn't spoken to Noam in months.

But then I thought better of it, realizing my instinct was really more of a reflex, like when the doctor hits your knee with a hammer and your leg jumps. It took me a second to register all of this, and it was very strange to just let him go but I realized it was the right thing to do. It was sort of a profound moment because that singular act was so loaded. And even though it broke my heart, my just letting Noam walk away made me realize that I really *had* let him go.

I realized, too, that Hanna had been right all along. Despite the fact that she had made a string of bad decisions in her own life, she was still capable of giving me very good advice: you can never move forward if you still have one leg in the past.

It occurred to me in that moment, as well, that part of why I'd been holding on to Nico was because I couldn't hold on to Noam and maybe a psychologist (a halfway decent one, anyway) would have told me I was transferring my emotion from one situation to the next. Maybe it was easier to be obsessed with Nico and go psycho from that than to deal with the loss of Noam.

They say if you don't deal with your shit in one relationship, you're just going to repeat it in your next one. Regardless of what would or would not happen with Guy, I was planning on dealing with my life from here on out with a very clear head.

Time moved forward, as it is wont to do, and Guy's visit eventually rolled around. Soon enough it was December and I was on my way to the airport to pick him up. Although we talked on the phone fairly frequently I hadn't seen him in more than two months and I began to think that it was entirely possible I had completely lost my mind. What in the world would we do for *sixteen* days in the dead of a New York winter, trapped in my tiny apartment? It's one thing to have a love affair in a foreign country. It's another story entirely to invite someone into your home—especially when your home is the size of a rabbit cage. The only thing I had to go off of was how I felt while I was with him when I was in Israel. It was not lost on me that it was entirely possible that my fondness for Guy could have been brought on by some sort of sex- and pheromone-induced state of mind.

Because I am a total narcissist, I am constantly seeking instant gratification. On account of this, I often get really excited about something and then when I've found something that I think might gratify me more or better or more quickly, I lose all interest in the first thing.

It's not like this hadn't happened to me before. The worst might have been back in college when David Grosenschmidt came to Arizona to visit me. David and I had met in Florence during our semesters abroad. Instead of all the Italian men I could have had a love affair with, I wound up sleeping with a Jew with a big nose from Long Island. At some point I found out that he had a girlfriend back home, the daughter of a mustard heiress, and I promptly broke up with him—at which point he declared his love for me and swore to me that he had broken it off with the mustard heiress. I took him back and we resumed our affair for the duration of our time in Italy. I was really into David, until he got off the plane when he came to visit me in Arizona.

The second I saw him and his big nose and his thin, wispy hair, I was completely revolted. I couldn't even look at him, let alone have sex with him. I believed that all the gluttony of the pasta and the wine and the pot I had been smuggling from Amsterdam had clouded my judgment. Or, more likely, it was the fact that in the time that had passed, and in David's absence, I had met and become smitten with someone else. Or maybe it was just that even though I had enjoyed him in Italy it didn't necessarily mean I was going to like him in America. All of this is to say I had no idea how I would feel about Guy when I saw him in New York and I was not looking forward to a repeat of that experience. I don't mind making mistakes. I just like to think that I actually learn from them.

I braced myself as I walked into the airport.

And the second I saw Guy, I *knew*. He walked out into the airport with a backpack and he looked like such a tourist and he was so cute and had come so far just to see me. It all came flooding back. When I hugged him, it was absolutely electric. Even after eleven hours on a plane, surrounded by hot, sweaty Middle Easterners, he smelled delicious.

We were both a little nervous in the taxi to my place and when we arrived he seemed kind of tripped out by my crazy

Chinese whorehouse building. But by the time we got upstairs and he saw how cute and cozy and neat and clean the apartment was, I could tell he calmed down.

I gave him a glass of wine and was like, "Well, do you have them?"

Guy: "Yes, I do."

Me: "In *English*?"

Guy: "*Yes, in English.*"

Me: "Well, can I see them?"

Guy went fishing around in his carry-on and pulled out an envelope and handed it to me.

Me: "Thank you."

I opened the envelope and was pleased to see that he was officially not HIV positive.

You may think this is psychotic, but I'll be real fucking clear here. No one and I mean *no one* is sticking his dick in me without a condom without my seeing some hard evidence that he is not infected with some disease. Men are dogs and like dogs, they need papers. And any woman who doesn't require this from a guy is a fucking idiot. If you're too shy to ask or if you think he's not going to like you anymore, I have two things to say: (1) if he doesn't like you enough to get tested for STDs, then you shouldn't be fucking him to begin with, and (2) men are willing to do pretty much anything to get laid.

I was like, "This is great news. Mazel tov. There's just one more thing we need to get out of the way."

A look of consternation crossed his face.

"We are going to be stuck in this tiny apartment for sixteen days so we really can't afford to get caught up in formalities," I said as I handed him a book of matches. "I only have one bathroom."

That sufficiently broke the ice and for the next two days the only time we stopped having sex was to sleep and eat. After we had fucked so many times that I could barely walk (not that I was complaining), I took Guy traipsing around Manhattan. Even though we went to places I have been to a thousand times, just being with him made it all exciting. I mean, being with him was exciting to begin with, but being with him and watching how excited he was to be with me and in New York was even more exciting. Plus, he was hot and I was horny, which even made things like riding the subway fun. He was so interested in every little thing and he noticed things I had never even paid attention to—buildings, parks, stores, architecture. It was like I was discovering the world with him anew. Plus, it was Christmastime in New York, so the city was even more majestic than usual.

I started to think that perhaps I had not been delusional at all. I started to think that I actually really, really liked him. In fact, I was becoming kind of crazy about him. He was almost too good to be true. He was sweet and thoughtful, he made me coffee in the morning, he cooked, he cleaned, he smelled delicious, he fucked me until I couldn't even see straight, and he cracked me up. He was interested in music and art and good food and wine and on top of that he was incredibly snuggly.

Moreover, because he had no reference point for anything I was talking about, sharing my idiosyncrasies with him was amazing because his reactions were priceless. I felt like I was living in a comedy sketch.

For example, when I tried to share my love for Ice-T and his wife, Coco, I asked Guy, "Do you know Ice-T and Coco?"

And Guy said, in his hilarious accent, "Yes, I like iced tea and *chocco*."

Chocco is the word for cocoa (chocolate milk) in Hebrew.

I was *dying*. I was like, "Not *that* iced tea and cocoa! Don't you know Ice-T and Coco?!"

I showed Guy a bunch of pictures of Ice-T and he did, indeed, recognize him. He said, "Oh yes, he makes rap music."

I was like, "Yes! He does make rap music. Ice-T is the OG!"

I could tell by the expression on Guy's face that he had no clue what I was talking about.

I was like, "OG, Original Gangster. Ice-T is like the godfather of hip-hop. He's very important, culturally speaking."

Guy was like, "Okay, but then what is this Coco?"

I showed Guy a litany of images of Coco with her huge boobs and bubble butt in a variety of fluorescent g-strings. He was finally like, "I get it! Who is *that*?"

Me: "That's Coco. She's Ice-T's wife!"

Guy, in his adorable broken English: "She is singer like him?"

Me: "No."

Guy: "So why she is famous?"

Me: "Well, she's kind of a model and actress but she's also famous for her camel toe."

Guy: "What is camel *too*?"

I was bowled over at this point. I was like, "Not camel *too*, camel *toe*." And then I pulled my jeans up as far as I could and showed him how my vagina was divided in half by the fabric and it looked like a camel's toe.

And Guy said, "Oy yoy yoy. I thought maybe you say she is famous for music or because she make art. But no, she is famous for camel toe. Only in this stupid country can someone be famous for camel toe."

I snuggled up next to him and pulled up my favorite video on

YouTube, which is an interview with Ice-T where he talks about meeting Coco. They were on the set of a music video (he was wearing a red sharkskin suit) and he saw Coco and went right up to her and said, "Hey, baby, would you ever consider dating a gangster rapper?"

And she cooed, "Well, if he was niiiiiice."

Ice replied, "If you take the *N* from N-I-C-E you get Ice."

I started clapping. I was like, "I *love* that story! It's so romantic!"

Guy looked at me like I was crazy.

Me: "Do you get it?"

Guy: "Yes, I get it. If you take the *N* from N-I-C-E you get Ice-T."

And then he gave me a kiss on my forehead and told me I should be committed to a mental institution.

Right then, I decided: I love this boy.

And then we had our first fight.

It went down like this: Guy was trying to tell me that he loved having sex with me. But because he is a man, and men are retarded, instead of just saying *that*, he launched into some story about some girl he used to date who was crazy but also "really hot" and other than the fact that she was crazy, she couldn't have an orgasm. The combination of the two, apparently, were real turnoffs and thus he dumped her.

This story made me feel homicidal. I have never been a jealous person, but I was actually seeing red. I was like, "First of all, I don't know why you think I'm interested in hearing about girls you used to have sex with. Why would you even tell me that story? Are you trying to make me jealous? Do you want me to tell you the story about how I used to have sex with a twenty-four-year-old Dolce and Gabbana model? Would that be an interesting story for you to hear?"

Guy looked at me like I had lost my mind, which perhaps I had.

I continued, "What? You *don't* want to hear about how I used to fuck a really hot twenty-four-year-old Dolce and Gabbana model?"

Guy was like, "Okay, okay. Enough. I get it."

I was like, "That's good. I'm glad you get it because I can't tell you how little interest I have in hearing about how you've fucked really hot girls. I have news for you. *I've* fucked really hot girls, too. And if you keep it up, there's a really cute hotel around the corner and you're more than welcome to stay there."

Thankfully, it didn't come to that.

A few nights later at my favorite Italian restaurant, over a glass of wine and homemade fettuccini with ragu sauce, he said it again. This time straight to my face: "I love you."

But this time he didn't preface it with "I think."

So while all of this was very intense, it was also really refreshing and part of what I liked so much about Guy. He wasn't afraid to tell the truth—even if it was scary or crazy or made him vulnerable. He was very up-front about, well, everything.

He was also super laid-back about pretty much everything and other than that one fight, being with him was just *easy.*

My parents, of course, wanted to meet him. At least my mother did. She was all up in my shit about it, too. I suppose I could understand that after the year of insanity I had been through she was dying to see what I'd gotten myself wrapped up in. I wasn't so sure I was ready for this—if for no other reason than just the sheer fact that I didn't want to deal with a barrage of questions.

I knew my mother would love Guy. I wasn't so sure about what my father would think. On a good day my father was doing you a favor if you managed to get more than a sentence out of him. But he had spent a good deal of time in Israel for work and he had a soft spot for Israelis. Plus, they actually sort of had a lot in common. They were both really into sports and they'd both served in the army. And they were both kind of quiet no-nonsense kind of guys, but once you got them going they had a really dry sense of humor and were actually really funny.

When I told Guy my parents wanted to meet him, he was like, "Okay. Let's go meet them."

I was way more apprehensive. In my world, introducing someone to your parents was a big deal. To begin with, it has all sorts of implications and I still wasn't sure what this relationship was or where it was going—if it were going anywhere at all. As crazy as my parents drive me, they're pretty much the most important people in my life and I didn't want to introduce them to someone who was not going to be around for a long time. Plus, I knew I was going to have to field a million questions from my mother. And at this point, as into him as I was, there was really no way to know anything. I mean we were having a blast and we totally adored each other, but we lived like six thousand miles apart.

But Israeli culture is very family-oriented and Guy was so casual about the whole thing that I acquiesced. Before I did, though, I was like, "For the last time, are you *sure* you want to meet them?"

And Guy said, "Well, I'm going to meet them at some point, so why not now?"

I wasn't sure where he was going with that, but his nonchalance was reassuring.

Uncle Bark was having a Chanukah party and my entire family was going to be there. I figured with so many people there it was a safe bet that we could get in and out within an hour and with minimal damage.

Uncle Bark, who is charming under pretty much any circumstance, was mildly intoxicated from his white wine spritzer when we got there and was as amusing as ever. The second we walked in, Uncle Bark came over and started talking to us in broken Hebrew. But the person Guy got along with more than anyone was my father. My father, whom you usually have to beat over the head to get him to talk, was in the corner with Guy, chatting away for the better part of an hour. After a while I sidled up to them to investigate what they were going on about. What else? Sports. Or more to the point, sportswear. Specifically, sneakers. My father, who has been playing paddleball (like handball, but more street) religiously since he was in his twenties, is completely obsessed with sneakers. Because my father has an obsessive personality, the man owns more sneakers than even Shaquille O'Neal would need for a lifetime. I'm talking in the hundreds. In Israel, which is a tiny country the size of Rhode Island, huge sporting goods stores don't exist. So when Guy discovered them in New York, it was like a dream come true. When my father then offered to take Guy to Modell's, the biggest sneaker store on the planet, I knew it was all over.

My mother eventually made her way over and started talking our ears off. She asked Guy, "So, what's your favorite thing about New York?"

Guy said, wholly and without reservation, "Periel."

Between that and his newly found best friend in my father, my mom was totally sold.

After we left, Guy took my hand, and was like, "Where did you come from? Your parents are so nice and you're, well, such a . . . little monster."

One of my favorite things about Guy was that he says what he means and he means what he says. That and he always does what he says he is going to do. You can also always count on him to say what he thinks. This I could sometimes do without. This may have been a cultural phenomena, but whatever it was, Guy had no filter.

Once, for example, right after we had sex doggy style, he said, "You are very sexy and I love you but the hair in your ass is so long I could braid it."

Who says that?

A girl less self-confident than I am would have probably never had sex again. And while it was true that maybe I had gone a bit more au naturel, I wasn't sure about the braiding part. Beyond that, Guy wasn't a gorilla but he certainly had his fair share of fur.

I was as mortified as I was amused. I was like, "You are *such* a misogynist."

Guy said, "A what?"

I was like, "Never mind. Hang on."

I hopped off the bed and bent over in front of the mirror to investigate my anus. He actually wasn't that far off. I was like, "Well, whatever. I may have some hair in my butt but I've never had any complaints and before you start talking about my ass, you should look at your own!"

Guy said, "I'm a man. I'm supposed to have hair on my body."

I said, "That is a social construct that you've been brainwashed to think is the natural order."

Then it took me an hour to explain to Guy what misogyny and social constructs and the natural order were. And if you think that's a task for the faint of heart, you are sadly mistaken. Finally he got it but still maintained that he felt like he was having sex with a goat.

Later, I found a shoe box on my desk with a Post-it on top and thought, *How cute, a gift.* Guy had taken to leaving me Post-it notes all over the apartment—little notes that said "I love you" or whatever and I thought this was a more sophisticated version of that. When I got closer, I noticed that instead of saying "I love you," the Post-it said "ASS KIT."

When I opened the box, there was a can of hairspray, a brush, and a hair dryer.

(Of course I didn't tell him this, but I thought this was hands-down one of the most brilliant things I had ever seen in my life.)

On the flip side, I knew I could always count on him to tell me the truth—which, as my grandmother used to say, is nothing to sneeze at. Plus, I appreciated his sense of humor. I could tell him anything and we always had a great time together. Other than the fact that he lived in the Middle East and I lived in North America, everything was perfect. Or, perhaps, everything was perfect precisely *because* he lived in the Middle East and I lived in North America.

We went back and forth like this—I would go to Israel; he would come to New York—for about a year. At which point things changed. The complete abandon had been replaced with caution. Things were getting serious and the reality that we lived on different continents had sunk in. Of course, the reality that

I had fallen in love with him had also begun to sink in. Summer was coming and it was time to put on my big-girl pants and make some decisions.

I had always wanted to live in Israel and now seemed like as good a time as ever. I knew that no one ever accomplished anything in this world without taking a chance. But knowing something and actually doing something are two very different animals. I had just spent the better part of the year building my little nest. Was I really going to put all my stuff in storage and sublet my apartment? And what about work? I came up with a million scenarios. On the other hand, was I really going to *not* do something I had been dying to do for my whole life so I could sit in New York and babysit my pink couch? What it came down to was the only reason *not* to go to Israel for the summer was because I was scared.

That sealed the deal. Making decisions out of fear was not only the worst way to make decisions; it was also pathetic. And I may have been a lot of things, but pathetic was no longer one of them.

Plus, in the scheme of things, what was three months?

I thought Guy would be thrilled when I told him I was coming to Israel for the summer, but instead he sounded concerned. Guy, who as a general rule was much more practical than I was, started going through a list of "what ifs."

What would I do all day while he was at work?

What if I didn't like living in Israel?

What if I didn't like him?

What if things didn't work out?

What would I do on Monday nights when he played soccer?

On and on it went. But the underlying concern was clear. How would this relationship ever really work when we lived on separate continents? And furthermore, what if it didn't?

As far as I was concerned, I knew I would never forgive myself if I didn't give it a shot. But I understood Guy's position as well. A relationship with me was way out of left field for him. He may have been well traveled and well educated and sophisticated in a certain way—he appreciated fine food and fine wine and film and music and art—but for the most part he was a much more conventional and practical person than I was. He was more responsible than I was. He was less reactionary. He had a good job. He saved money. He visited his parents every Friday. He played soccer every Monday. He played poker every Thursday. He didn't drive if he drank. If he took a trip, he *planned* it. He used a condom. I mean not with me, but whatever. Naturally, some of this was just pure common sense. But the point is that when Guy made decisions, he thought them through.

I was more like a caveman—far from practical, totally unconventional and entirely self-indulgent. I made decisions on a whim. I spent more money than I had. I decided everything at the very last minute. I mean I wasn't an idiot but I was much less measured. In short, Guy's superego was in charge of his life and my id was in charge of mine. And although he was madly in love with me, this aspect of my personality scared the shit out of him.

He told me he needed a couple of days to think about it.

This simultaneously totally freaked me out and made me completely irate. I toyed with the idea of holding out for his "decision." Then, at like two in the morning, I decided that I had zero interest in waiting a couple of days or, frankly, even a couple of hours. So I wrote him an e-mail. I briefly considered the possibility that perhaps I should stop writing letters to men who want nothing to do with me trying to convince them otherwise.

Then I hit SEND.

Guy,

There are no guarantees in life. It doesn't matter how long you take to think or how much you try to plan, you have no way of knowing how our relationship is going to work out and neither do I.

This summer things may be wonderful. Or they may not. There are a million other things that could happen, too. You can't figure out the future.

I understand your concerns but you are NOT responsible for my choices. I make my own decisions and I live with what happens. You are NOT responsible if things don't work out between us.

I know you're scared. It's okay. Life can be scary.

You can live your life not taking risks and making decisions out of fear but I don't think that really protects you from anything.

I will say this: I want to be with someone who KNOWS they want to be with me. I want to be with someone who is THRILLED to see me, not with someone who is not sure. And when you say you need a couple of days to think about it, it makes me think that you're not sure.

And so in a way, I only need one answer from you: do you want to see me?

Yes or no.

A lot of things are not black-and-white, but this is.

You are either willing to walk away from this and risk never seeing me again because you are scared or you're willing to take a chance. It's the summer, honey. It's not a huge deal. It is supposed to be fun and exciting and wonderful. And maybe a little bit scary and maybe even a little bit boring.

We can figure out what we want to do after when the summer is over. We can't figure it out now. But if I don't come, we will never know. I don't want to do that. I'm not willing to live my life never taking risks because I'm scared. Are you?

Another thing that is black-and-white is this: I love you.

And then I went to sleep.

When I woke up the next morning, which also happened to be Guy's birthday, I rolled out of bed to check my e-mail and braced myself.

Guy had e-mailed me back, which was a good sign. It was a short e-mail, written in Hebrew, so it took me a few minutes to read it.

It said:

You coming to Israel for the summer would be the best birthday present I could have ever hoped for. I love you.

By nightfall, I had purchased a ticket to Israel, sublet my apartment, and spent hours online looking for a place to live in Tel Aviv. Since I was planning to spend the majority of my time writing, I had several requirements: the apartment had to be walking distance from the beach and it had to have a balcony. On Craigslist of all places, I found an American expat from New York City named Maya Silver, who had just moved in with her boyfriend. She had a one-bedroom apartment, dead smack in the center of the city, two blocks from the beach, with a balcony.

I was thrilled. I called Guy to tell him and I thought he would be thrilled as well. Wrong again. The way he saw it, if

I were coming to Israel, in essence to be with *him*, I should be staying *with* him. The way I saw it, this was the worst idea I had ever heard in my life. I explained to him that hanging out with someone on your own terms is *fun* but that living with someone is a nightmare. I also said that given the fact that your primary concern is that you don't want to be responsible for me, I'm pretty certain that moving in together more or less guarantees a disaster. Plus, I told him, no offense but I don't *want* to live with you. It's too much pressure.

He begrudgingly accepted this but I could tell his macho Middle Eastern ego was bruised.

I closed the deal with Maya Silver and leased her apartment for two months. Then I called to break the news to my mother.

I was like, "Hi, Mommy, I just want to let you know that I'm going to Israel for the summer."

To which my mother replied: "I just read an article in the *New York Times*. No one wants to get into a relationship with someone who is not financially stable. The article says it's not a good way to start a relationship."

Me: "Well, living over five thousand miles apart is not a good way to start a relationship either. Did you ever think of that? And really! Do you always have to be so negative!?"

My mother: "I am *not* negative. I am very optimistic, but unlike you I don't live in a fantasy world."

Me: "I don't know why you can't say something normal, like 'have a nice trip.'"

My mother: "And make sure you wear cotton clothing on the flight."

Me, now screaming: "Mommy, what the fuck are you talking about? What kind of a thing is that to tell me?"

My mother: "Language, Peri! Language!"

Me: "Seriously, are you insane? Who do you work for the FAA?"

My mother: "Cotton is less flammable than polyester so if something happens, it's much safer."

Me: "I am hanging up now. Please don't ever call me again."

This scared the living shit out me. I hate flying to begin with and if there is anything that I hate more than flying it is people who tell you scary stories about flying.

Within moments, I received this e-mail:

You don't know how lucky you are to be leaving shortly for Israel.

You must enjoy the melodramatic insane yelling that is becoming a habit with you. I was repeating constructive advice that was broadcast on national television from SURVIVORS of plane crashes. They were not hurt because they knew exactly where the emergency doors were and they wore natural fiber clothing.

And don't tell me that I was wrong because you are afraid. If you were not in denial and mature you would stop smoking. Statistics show how much more hazardous smoking, driving, and just walking are than flying.

You make up your own rules and treat me as if I am an imbecile. Grow up and be respectful and responsible; it's about time you act as a mature adult and not a teenager.

If you think this is harsh criticism, then believe me when I tell you that if you were not going on a trip it would be much more, so consider yourself lucky.

And if this has to do with your PMS, then we need to address that also.

I have to make a lunar calendar of your mood swings.

Love,
Mommy

Lucky for me, I got to Israel safely and my flight did not catch on fire. Also lucky for me is that the apartment I rented from Maya Silver was large and airy and two blocks from the beach. It was a bit filthy though, and Guy cleaned the entire thing the second he saw it. And when I say cleaned, I mean, like, with a mop.

I was like, "I don't know why we're not calling a cleaning lady. Just so you know, I don't do manual labor."

Guy sneered at me, finished mopping, and lectured me on how if I'd asked *before* I rented the apartment whether it was going to be cleaned, I wouldn't have problems like these. The way I saw it, the only problem I had was that Guy was being a fucking asshole. He was obviously still pissed I wouldn't move in with him and he was also obviously still conflicted about the fact that I was there at all.

As the days and weeks went on, it became more and more apparent that he was still apprehensive about the whole thing. His apprehension made me reticent to put myself too much on the line, so I became guarded and buried myself in my writing. And when he called, I often didn't answer and would only call him back hours later. I wasn't trying to play games as much as I was trying to be cautious. If he didn't want to be responsible for me that was fine, but I certainly wasn't going to be at his disposal. As a result, a rift grew between us.

In the midst of this, Hanna came to visit for a week. Her

trip to India had inspired her to travel more and I was thrilled to see her. We gallivanted around Israel, we took a trip to Jordan, and we even rode a camel. I barely saw Guy at all while Hanna was there. The day after she left, I had plans with him. We spent the evening together and then, later that night, while we were in bed, I said to him, "You know, I've been here for almost three weeks and you haven't told me once that you're happy that I'm here."

Guy said, "I am happy you're here, but . . ."

I was like, "But what?"

Guy said, "Well, I'm just not sure."

I bolted out of bed and started getting dressed.

He said, "Where are you going?"

I go, "You're not *sure?* You're not sure and you're asking me where I'm going? Where do you think I'm going? I'm going *home*. Do you really think I'm going to spend one single solitary second with someone who is *not sure* if they want to be with me!"

As I stormed out of his apartment, he handed me my make-up bag and said, "You forgot this."

I slammed the door. I was so livid I was seething. With the exception of my little "I'm not that girl" tantrum with Nico, which had provided me with sufficient humiliation for a lifetime, I had never stormed out like that on anyone before. I walked to the street and at one in the morning, I hailed a taxi back to my apartment and called Hanna, who had literally just arrived back in New York.

I told her what just happened and I was like, "I'm getting the fuck out of here. I can't believe what a moron I am. I'm getting on the next plane to JFK."

Hanna: "P, you know you will never forgive yourself if you do that."

Me, ranting: "He's not sure? He's not fucking sure? He can go fuck himself if he's not sure. I am not going to fucking be with someone who is not sure!"

Hanna: "Slow down for a second. Can I ask you a question?"

Me: "What?"

Hanna: "Are *you* sure? Are you one hundred percent positive?"

Me, meekly: "Well, no. Of course not."

Hanna: "Well then."

Me: "Well then, what?"

Hanna: "Well then you need to go back."

Me: "Go back? Are you out of your fucking mind?"

Hanna: "You have to go back and apologize. You're being insane."

Me: "Well, if that's not the pot calling the kettle black."

Hanna: "P, this isn't about me. And you know that."

I decided to sleep on it, which was hopeless. I tossed and turned all night and the next morning, at about seven, I put my bruised ego and my sorry ass *back* into a taxi and went *back* to Guy's apartment and sniveled an apology to him. Guy, as was the norm for him, was fairly stoic about the whole thing. A few days later, he said he wanted to meet for dinner so we could "discuss" our relationship.

Anytime you have to discuss your relationship, you know you're in trouble. No one ever gets together to discuss a relationship if everything is going well. No one's ever like, "Hey, I wanted to talk to you about our relationship because I think it's going really well." If you get together with someone to discuss your relationship, it's most likely because your relationship is fucked.

Over dinner, Guy told me that he really liked me but that

he just wasn't "sure" about us. He also said that he really didn't think I was putting one hundred percent into our relationship. When I didn't respond, he asked me, "Are *you* putting one hundred percent into this relationship?"

The truth, of course, was that I wasn't putting one hundred percent into this relationship at all. The truth, of course, was that I was so preoccupied with making sure I didn't get hurt that I was fucking the whole thing up. But it was too late to do anything about that. The only thing I could do, it seemed, was at least get out of this with my dignity intact. So instead of blowing myself up like a suicide bomber, which was what I wanted to do, I told him the truth. He was right, I said. I hadn't been putting one hundred percent into our relationship. I told him that I, too, wasn't sure if this was a one-night stand that we had mistaken for something else, but that I definitely felt something for him that I couldn't explain away. He seemed really conflicted and we decided it was probably best to take some time apart.

Or, rather, *he* decided it would be good to take some time apart and I agreed. But I agreed mostly because I knew I had no choice. If I had learned anything at all, it was that if someone wasn't sure if they wanted to be with you the worst thing you can do is to try to convince them otherwise. They'll just retreat further. It's human nature. You can't force things and if Guy was ambivalent, then so be it. I told him I hoped he would come around, and more than that, I hoped that if he *did* come around that I would still feel the same way.

I was proud of myself. It takes strength to be vulnerable. We had a sweet and very sad parting that night. We hugged for a while and I went back to Maya Silver's apartment knowing that at the very least I had been honest, and that was really all I could do.

The next day I had resigned myself to the fact that things very likely were just not going to work out between us and I was going to have to live with that.

And then I got a text message from him as though nothing had happened. He had the gall—the audacity really—to invite me to go to his *parents'* house with him for lunch. Like we hadn't pretty much just broken up the night before.

Now I was really confused. And pissed. What the fuck?

I wrote back saying that given our conversation the night before, I really didn't think it was a good idea, at all, and that perhaps it would be best to see each other when he was more clear on how he felt and what he wanted.

The whole thing was beginning to seem very insane to me.

I called Roy and told him what was going on. I was like, "I don't know what his deal is, but I am not in the mood for mind games."

Roy was like, "I don't know what's going on with the two of you, but I can tell you for sure that Guy is not the type of person to fuck around and if he's asking you to go to his parents' house with him, you should just go."

Meanwhile, Guy would not stop texting me.

So I caved.

From the moment he picked me up, everything was different. *He* was different. I felt like I was in *The Twilight Zone*. I don't know if he had been testing me the night before or if the fact that I had been so honest had lessened his fear or if my willingness to be vulnerable made him feel less vulnerable or if it was a combination of all of the above. Or maybe it was that he had told his parents I was coming for lunch and he didn't want to show up without me. I knew his parents adored me but that seemed like kind of a stretch.

Whatever it was, it seemed insane.

When I called him out on his erratic Dr. Jekyll/Mr. Hyde behavior, he got all *verklempt*. I got a sense that I had really done his head in. I was in Israel but I wasn't staying with him. My friend came and I went away with her. I didn't answer the phone. Was I coming or going or staying? When I pressed him on this, he said, "Your lease is up in two weeks and I think you should move in with me."

I remained silent.

For the next two weeks, from morning until night, I sat outside at the coffee shop across the street from my apartment and wrote. Guy came by to say hi almost every day. He left work and drove the fifteen minutes across town just to give me a kiss or bring me flowers. The first time he brought flowers to the coffee shop, he texted me and told me he was parked up the block and to just leave my stuff and come meet him. When I got to the car, he handed me a bouquet of flowers and said, "I couldn't bear to be one of those pathetic guys who gives you flowers in public, but I hope your writing is going well and I can't stay but I just wanted to tell you that I love you."

As the summer and my lease drew to an end, it became increasingly clear that I was going to have to make some sort of very serious decision.

The way I saw it, I had three options:

1. Renew my lease at Maya Silver's.
2. Go back to New York.
3. Move in with Guy.

After living with Noam for ten years, the last thing I wanted to do was play house. Moving in with someone was serious business and moving out was even *more* serious business. I asked myself if I was really ready to get that serious.

I knew that there were, of course, no guarantees with anything in life, but the thought of going through yet *another* breakup made me want to toss myself into oncoming traffic. On the other hand, I felt like I had been standing at the edge of the diving board for quite some time and it was time to jump or go home.

I jumped.

13

THE ONE I'VE BEEN WAITING FOR

On August 1, 2009, I moved into Guy's apartment. It had been nearly a year to the day we met. The first thing I did was throw away every single trinket in it. The second thing I did was throw away the god-awful painting he had hanging over the couch. Then I reorganized the entire apartment. Guy was a clean freak but his organizational skills were for the birds and his "taste" in design was haphazard at best. I don't do floors or windows or really anything of that ilk but I am totally OCD and will organize the shit out of any closet, cabinet, or drawer. I also threw out all his sheets and towels and bought new ones. Things were coming together. At least in the apartment they were.

The adjustment of living in Israel was another story. I adored Guy and while Tel Aviv was a great city to visit, I found that it was not nearly as dynamic as New York when it came to actually living there. Moving someplace new was always exciting until you got used to the place and then it wasn't new anymore. And after the newness of Tel Aviv wore off, I started to get really claustrophobic.

Guy was really cute and he tried really hard to make me feel at home; he left me little notes telling me how much he loved me and he took me to the beach at night and he was very romantic— all the time. He was always hugging me and kissing me and he was obsessed with music, so he was constantly dedicating songs to me.

We could be in the middle of anything and he would suddenly stop everything and say, "This song is dedicated to you . . ." He liked dark, brooding stuff like Nick Cave and Leonard Cohen and he was obsessed—*obsessed*—with Neil Young. I mean he was crazy, too, don't get me wrong. He took like five showers a day and was constantly cleaning shit but other than that and his occasional big mouth—which made me want to murder him— he was pretty much an angel. I mean, listen, no one's perfect.

I was writing all day but I was restless. I decided I needed to get a job. So I found a bartending gig. I had bartended on and off for years in New York but I quickly learned that bartending in Tel Aviv was very different from bartending in New York. Bartending in New York is awesome. Bartending in Tel Aviv, not so much. For starters, in New York there is something called *tips*. This was a concept that had apparently not yet been integrated into Israeli society. Because I didn't drive, I was taking taxis to and from work and it was costing me as much in travel as I was making in a night. Moreover, because we were in Israel, everything was in Hebrew—from the cash registers to the menus to everything in between. I spoke Hebrew, but I didn't read Hebrew, so this was a nightmare as well.

Beyond that, I was like an indentured servant, scrubbing glasses and mopping floors until four in the morning. In addition to tips, restaurants and bars in New York have something called dishwashers. They were invented during the Industrial Revolution but apparently restaurants in Israel had not yet received this memo either. The glasses would be washed in the back and then they would be stacked in front of us and we had to dry them *by hand*. And then the manager, Shira, would come over and hold each one under the light as though she were appraising a rare gem. No matter how clean I would get the glasses, Shira would be like, "Are you sure you dried this glass? There are still some water spots on it."

And then, *she* would actually rinse a glass off and dry it in front of me and say, "This is what the glasses are supposed to look like when they are dry."

It wasn't long before I wanted to bash her face in. It was painfully obvious to me that Shira was overcompensating for the fact that she would be running that restaurant for the rest of her life. One day after I had been working there for a couple of months Shira came up to me and said, "I just want you to know that I really like you. I admire the fact that you came to a foreign country and I think you're really brave but I don't think this is really working out. What do you think?"

I said, "You really want to know what I think? I think you're a liar. You haven't liked me from the moment you met me and that's fine because I don't really like you either. Second of all, I think you're envious of the fact that for me this is a job and not a career. And third of all, when you grow up a little bit and get the owner's dick out of your ass, I think you will realize that your snotty attitude is a thinly veiled attempt to overcompensate for the fact that you are deeply insecure. That is what I think."

And with that, I collected the rest of my paltry salary and left.

After a few more months in Israel, I was really starting to get antsy. In Israel, I felt like I was a fish in a pond. And I didn't want to be a fish in a pond. I wanted to be a shark in the ocean. I was having delusions of grandeur and thinking of sharks when my phone rang and a number showed up I hadn't seen in months.

I said, "Your ears must have been ringing."

Nico said, "P?"

I said, "So funny you called. I was just thinking about sharks."

Nico said, "I'm doing well, thank you. How are you?"

I was like, "I'm good, but let's skip the formalities. What's going on?"

Nico said, "Well, actually, we just signed a new client and it's very up your alley and I thought maybe you'd want to be head creative on it."

In other words, he needed help. Given how we'd left things, it was shocking that he had the balls to call me out of the blue and ask me for help. I was about to articulate this when he said, "Given how we left things, I know it's really ballsy for me to call you out of the blue and ask you for help. And I would completely understand if you told me to go fuck myself and hung up . . . But it's a really big job."

And then he told me about it. It *was* a big job and it was also a very tempting offer. In many ways, there was nothing to think about. I wanted the job. I just wanted to make sure I'd be taking it for the right reasons. And then, too, it was as good an excuse as any to go back to New York.

Guy and I had been toying with the idea of going to New York for a while and this really did seem like the perfect opportunity. Guy was pretty much over his job anyway. It was a good job, a great job even, and though he never said it, I think meeting me made him realize that the world was full of possibilities he had never considered.

There was one thing I knew I had to do, which was to tell Guy about my history with Nico before we went to New York. Even though it was a moot point, I knew they would meet and I didn't want him to hear about it from someone else. Plus, I wanted to be completely honest with him. I was like, "Listen, this is totally irrelevant and it all happened a long time ago but I just wanted you to hear it from me. Nico and I used to kind of have a thing."

"And?" Guy asked.

I said, "And nothing. That's it."

To which Guy replied, "Mazel tov."

And with that, a few weeks later we were on our way back to New York.

One morning, shortly after we had arrived in New York, we were lazing about talking about how we had to move out of the rabbit cage and into a normal-size apartment when Guy said, "Let's go."

I was like, "Let's go where?"

Guy said, "Oy yoy yoy. Where else would we go? Let's go get a ring."

I got up and started pacing back and forth. I was like, "Seriously? You're making me very nervous right now."

Guy was like, "Well, that's your problem, not mine."

I eventually calmed down and we walked over to my favorite antiques shop, where he bought me a beautiful ring with *conflict-free* diamonds from 1916. Standing outside in the middle of Twenty-Fifth Street, I said, "*Well*, can I have it?"

And Guy said, "No, you can't *have* it. You have to agree to marry me first."

I was like, "Fine. Now can I have it?"

Guy shook his head. He was like, "There really is something wrong with you. You don't have a romantic bone in your body."

He took the ring out of its box and said, "So you'll marry me?"

I said, "Yes, yes, I'll marry you."

Later that night, he took a flower out of the vase on the kitchen table, took the ring *off* my finger, put on Nick Cave's "(Are You) The One That I've Been Waiting For?" and got down on his knee and again asked me to marry him.

And again, I said yes.

Epilogue

HAPPY ENDINGS

Noam and I eventually became very good friends again. We reunited when we had to put Eli, the dog we found so many years ago while we were eating Passover dinner, to sleep. It was an emotional reunion and I feel very lucky to still have him in my life. He lives in Brooklyn with his girlfriend, who works in human rights and who is probably far less vapid than I am.

Hanna met someone on her spiritual retreat in India. After a year of dating, she left Manhattan and they got a place together in Montana. He is a social worker and the opposite of every guy she has ever tried to date, i.e., he's not rich and he's not an asshole. She recently called me and said, "I got a massage yesterday with Ben and it really made me miss those happy endings. But then I told him all about them and he said he would be cool with it if I wanted to do that again. I think this time I might try it with a girl."

Nico and I made amends and went back to being best friends. He even helped me plan my wedding.

Guy and I got married in New York City on September 5, 2010. I refused to deal with anyone in the wedding industry, which is, by the way, the most insidious industry in the world. My dress was by Monique Lhuillier and I found it in the Gilda Radner Thrift Store on Seventeenth Street. It had been donated by a rich lady from the Upper East Side who bought it for her daughter who then decided she didn't want it. It was unworn, with the tags still on. The original price was $6,000.00. I paid $350.00. My shoes were by the late great Alexander McQueen. They were bright-red spike heels with a heart-shaped peep toe. The original price was $895.00. I bought them on sale for 75 percent off. *Just saying*. Hanna, incidentally, was my maid of honor.

Guy and I moved out of the rabbit cage to a loft. I took the couch that accompanied me on the journey described in this book with us until Guy finally convinced me to get rid of it, which I did begrudgingly. Literally one week after I donated it to a thrift store in the East Village, I got a phone call from my editor, Denise, to discuss the cover of my book. She said, "I know we had planned a different direction entirely, but one of my colleagues had an idea that everyone loves and I hope you'll be open to it because I think it could be really great."

I was like, "Go on."

Denise said, "We think you should be photographed on your grandmother's couch . . . If you still have it."

I was like, "You have *got* to be kidding me."

And then I told her the story.

We actually had to purchase the couch *back* from the thrift store so that we could use it for the cover shoot and then re-donate it. Since the plastic cover was long gone, I had to make about four thousand phone calls before I found a company in Queens, of all places, that would custom-make one for it.

I never found my hygienist Leslie Myron.

Uncle Bark is as crazy as ever. But he's one of my favorite people on the planet and I couldn't live without him.

Roy and his wife still live in Tel Aviv. They just had their second baby. He was the best man at our wedding.

Even though we left Chinatown, Guy and my father meet every single week (usually on Saturday mornings) to have coffee and get a foot massage around the corner from where we used to live.

My mother continues to be the best person on earth. She also continues to have absolutely no idea how funny she is.

If I have learned anything, it's that things don't work out the way you expect them to.

But sometimes they work out better. And your most important relationship is with yourself. And that hope, my friends, is a *verb*.

Acknowledgments

For a multitude of reasons, this truly would not have been possible without the following people. I am forever indebted: Doug Stewart, Denise Oswald, Cal Morgan, Carrie Kania, Jeanette Perez, Paula Cooper, Ken Siman, Kat Mattis, Stephanie Bonadio, Beth Silfin, and last but most certainly not least, Mia Tramz.

It's always nice to have a team of professionals at one's disposal. Thank you for helping me look and sound my very best: Mark Seliger, James Victore, Michael Angelo, Eli Evans, Ruth Levy, Rita Nakouzi, Mikhail Baryshnikov, and Jonathan Ames.

Were it not for all of you, I would have nothing to say: Kevin Greer, Ilana Arazie, Mark and Lisa Aschenbrand, Lori Barzvi, Adi and Ofer Miara, Roy and Merav Ron, Talma and Yochanan Ron, Sara and Dennis Belfor.

Behind the scenes, you guys really make it happen: Itay Koren, Ed Murphy, Jason Park, and James Gormley.

Honorable mention, thank you for your undying love and support: Vanessa Hamilton, Poppy King, Jenny Shimizu, Erica Medine, Mari Fujita, Eran Shakine, Stephanie Donahue, Jason Aschenbrand, Brette and Evan Aschenbrand, Camille Killian, Caroline Gates, and the one and only Herbert Lust.

My apologies and undying love: my parents, Eve and Michael Aschenbrand.

In Memory of
Guy Barzvi
(02/23/72 – 9/11/01)
&

My grandparents
Chana and Yerachmiel Wirnik
Lillian and Seymour Aschenbrand